THERE · ARE · NO COINCIDENCES

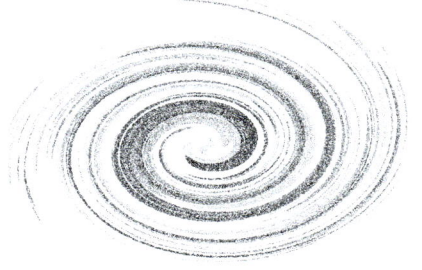

A L I Z A   K E L L Y

A MANIFESTATION DECK AND GUIDEBOOK

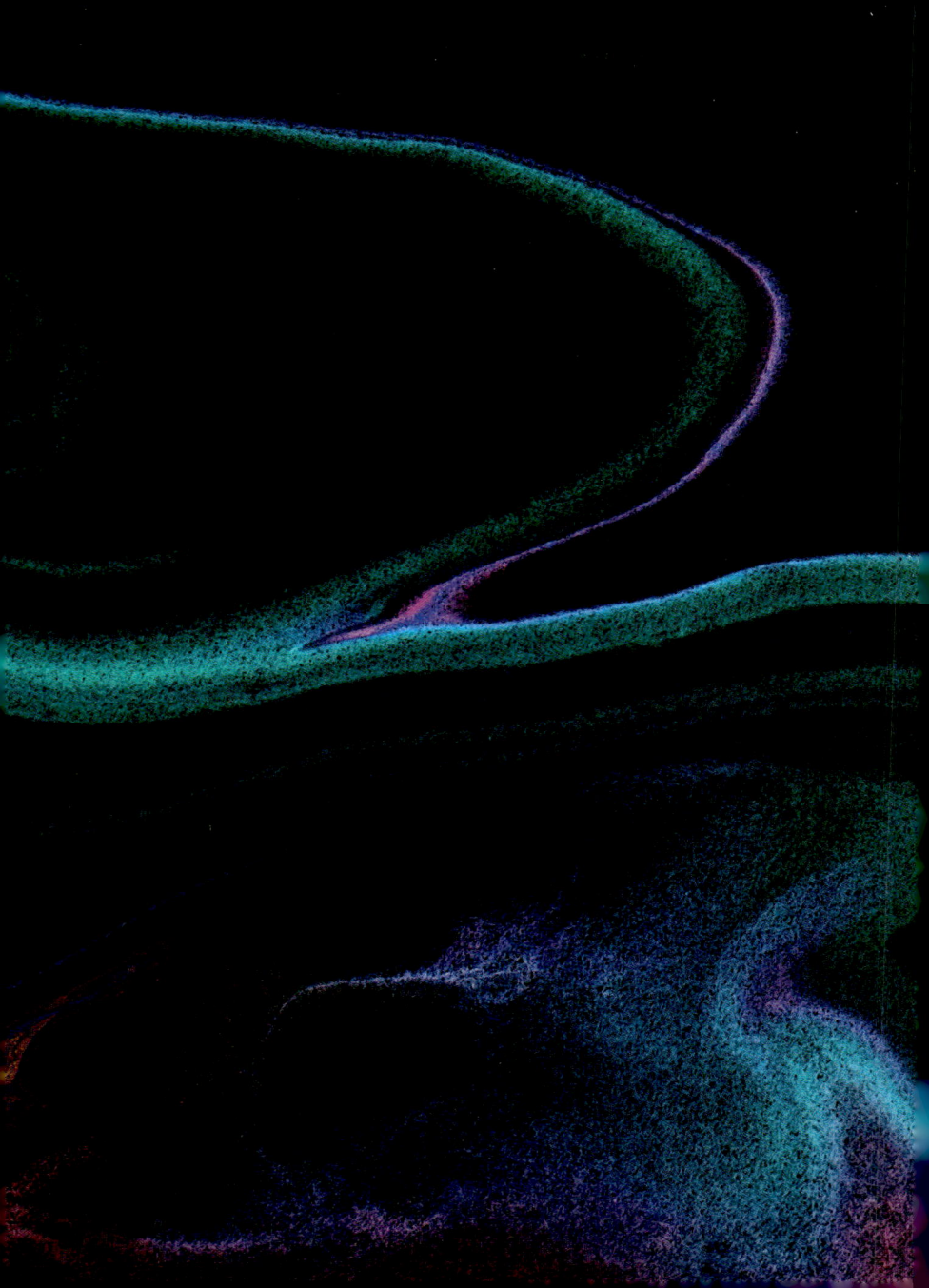

IT MEANS SOMETHING 4	TOTALITY AND VOIDS 6

THE ARCHITECTURE 7

| DESIGN
8 | KEYWORDS
74 | NUMBERS
9 |

TANC 75

| USING THE CARDS 76 | INTERPRETING THE CARDS 80 |

❋ ❋ ❋ ❋ ❋ ❋ ❋ ❋ **CATEGORIES** ❋ ❋ ❋ ❋ ❋ ❋ ❋ ❋ ❋

| COSMOS
11 | NATURE
27 |
| THRESHOLDS
43 | CHANCE
59 |

IT · MEANS SOMETHING

WHAT DOES IT MEAN WHEN YOU SEE 11:11?

Or when a hummingbird flutters by your window?

When you accidentally miss your flight?

Or experience an unforeseen chance encounter that has the potential to change your life forever?

Well, it means everything.

Every day, our existence is animated by infinite external and internal stimuli. Thoughts, smells, text message alerts. Barking dogs. Robotic callers. Bottomless memories. It's virtually *impossible* to process the extraordinary amount of data—by way of both real, tangible situations and extrasensory, energetic impressions—that inundates us on a day-to-day basis. Naturally, we choose how and where to focus our attention, prioritizing certain matters while simultaneously ignoring others. While this type of experiential triage is vital for emotional regulation (and we're evolutionarily wired to do it), there is a fine line between neutrality and neglect.

As we navigate the constant bombardment of breaking news tragedies and the back-to-back "unprecedented events" that have become a hallmark of our epoch, *in addition to* the stress, responsibilities, and exhaustion that affect us on an individual level, I fear that we—as a society—are becoming increasingly hardened and desensitized. And that calcification of detachment, the drone of dispassion, boredom—the dismissive shrug that accompanies "whatever, it doesn't matter"—has profound moral and ethical implications on the collective consciousness.

But what *is* the collective consciousness? Broadly speaking, the collective consciousness is the psyche of the macro—it's the beliefs, values, ethics, and morals that shape society at large. Although the extraordinary scale of the collective consciousness may feel insurmountable (after all, it's the amalgam of everyone and everything), from a mystical perspective, it's actually quite accessible. Metaphysical thought is rooted in the Hermetic axiom "as above, so below; as within, so without," which basically means that the micro and macro are inextricably linked. In other words, whatever principles apply to a whole (for instance, a country) also apply to its smaller parts (such as an apartment building). And, in accordance with this philosophy, your individual consciousness *is* the collective consciousness.

So, fundamentally, this is about *you*. No, really——it's personal. Your opinions, observations, decisions, emotions, and experiences play critical roles in the collective consciousness; in a sense, how you express your existence *defines* reality at large. The way you spend your time, money, energy, how you treat people——friends, relatives, as well as strangers on the Internet——all of it matters. All of it counts. All of it means something. Actions (and inactions) express convictions and, from a spiritual perspective, function as manifestations that reverberate across every dimension. Think of a human wave at a stadium concert or festival——hundreds of thousands of hands undulating in unison, creating a powerful electrical current of connectivity . . . and it all begins with a single gesture. That's you, right now.

There Are No Coincidences (TANC, for short) is both a statement and an expression. Used similarly to how "jinx" is exclaimed when two people accidentally say the same word or phrase in tandem, you may say "TANC" to call out those magickal synchronicities that we spiritually minded individuals know are much more than coincidence. For example, should you suddenly receive a text message from a person right as they popped into your mind——that's a TANC. Discovering that your current crush shares a birthday with your ex? TANC. Or that time you were rejected from what you thought was your dream job, only to proceed down a different path that ended up opening more doors than you could've ever imagined possible? TANC. Used as an exclamation, TANC signals deep spiritual awareness, because TANC is also a philosophy. Signs, symbols, and synchronicities are important because they underscore the significance of your existence; they matter because *you* matter. Strengthening your relationship with TANC—— that is, exploring sentience through pattern-recognition manifesting in both large and small ways——will deepen your appreciation of consciousness, enabling you to truly embody your monumental, albeit ineffable, value. The practice of TANC encourages you to not only acknowledge but actively *venerate* the sublime fortuity that is your existence . . . because everything you observe and all that you experience are microcosms designed to validate the macrocosm——the greatest TANC of all. You, my friend, are no coincidence.

THERE ARE NO COINCIDENCES

TOTALITY AND VOIDS

THERE ARE NO COINCIDENCES is a microcosm. The forty-four cards are divided into four sections—Cosmos, Nature, Thresholds, and Chance—with eleven cards in each group. Taken in its totality, this deck is intended to represent the macrocosm of every TANC that ever was, is, or will be. This is, of course, an impossible task. In the inconceivably expansive landscape that is symbolism, forty-four cards are barely a drop in the ocean. But in the wild world of mystical poetry, where ants and elephants dine at the same table, this deck should be regarded as complete.

Every card and its corresponding category was carefully selected to mirror the most frequent, pervasive, and ubiquitous TANCs I've encountered canonically—as in the stuff of myth and legend—as well as socially (through clients, students, friends, and family) and, of course, personally. Accordingly, my hope is that you will embrace this deck as a whole, calibrating each card to match the unique frequencies of your reality. If and when you discover the absence of a sign, symbol, or synchronicity that demands a role in this deck, invite an existing card to expand its reach—for instance, perhaps the Memories card includes rainbows, and the Animals also represents bones. My hope is that, within the inevitable confines of this deck, you will find limitless creative freedom, fortifying a harmonious connection, linking the space between the cards and the contours of your psyche.

THE ARCHITECTURE

WITHIN THIS DECK are boundless possibilities. As you familiarize yourself with *There Are No Coincidences*, the relationship you build with the cards——individually and as a whole——will be illuminated by special associations, correspondences, and experiences. Through time, you may discover that certain cards signify specific places, people, or events that are unique to your reality. That is, of course, no coincidence. Your bond with this special tool will, ultimately, transform into an extension of your consciousness: The cards' mystical insight is none other than your *own* wisdom, expressed through the language of signs, symbols, and synchronicities. And that, my friend, is the spirit of TANC.

Accordingly, this deck's architecture was engineered to foster boundless interpretation, divination, and creative expression. *There Are No Coincidences* is bolstered by sturdy foundational beams, but——like an open floor plan——you can organize, design, and modulate it in whatever way suits your workflow. You might enjoy dividing the deck into quadrants, as reflected through the four core categories. Perhaps you'll identify magickal patterns buried in each card's numerical classification. Or maybe you prefer a more open floor plan that reduces boundaries by emphasizing the deck's organic cyclicality, with each card cascading into the next like wall-less rooms in a modern-day mansion.

Remember, there is no hierarchy——one technique isn't better or worse than another. You have free range to experiment and explore the deck's myriad features, detailed below.

DESIGN

EVERY DETAIL OF *THERE ARE No Coincidences* was intentional. The fonts, backgrounds, colors, layouts, and iconography were rigorously calibrated to emit the special kind of magick most associated with found objects; like thumbing through forgotten texts at an old library, only to stumble upon a book so energetically charged it practically levitates off the shelf. Nostalgic yet totally unexpected, *There Are No Coincidences* is a bouquet of Victorian illustrations and 1970s psychedelia, anchored by the rigorous framework of an antique textbook. *There Are No Coincidences* was designed to foster brand-new perspectives on timeless archetypes, encouraging seekers to explore their realities——both what is known and yet to be discovered——through the poetics of limitless possibilities.

KEYWORDS

EACH CARD IS ILLUMINATED by four keywords intended to deepen your relationship with each sign, symbol, and synchronicity contained within the deck. These keywords offer insight, perspective, and nuance through comprehensive exploration——in fact, you may discover that, in many instances, a single card may express itself as auspicious and cautionary in tandem. This, of course, reflects the extraordinary dimensionality of every experience, an amalgam of exciting possibilities as well as unanticipated adjustments. Likewise, these keywords are designed to spark ideation. When working with the cards, consider how the keywords transform your understanding of TANC. Do these words and phrases strengthen your connection to the card? Do they expose specific details, dimensions, or dynamics that may not have been otherwise accessible? What additional concepts, narratives, or notions do these keywords conjure? As you continue fortifying your bond with the deck, you'll discover that these keywords serve as launching pads for continued interpretation, reflection, and analysis; I invite you to expand the definitions in accordance with your unique mystical practice.

NUMBERS

EACH CARD IS ASSIGNED A number, which anchors it both to its category and the deck's greater architecture. As you work with the deck, you'll discover that certain sequences mirror existing systems——for instance, the cards within Cosmos match the order of the celestial bodies in our galaxy, and the elements (Fire, Earth, Air, and Water) in the Nature section are organized per their astrological correspondences.

Other cards, however, were arranged through an intuitive process. After I created a handmade mock-up deck, I discovered that——like mysterious magnets——the signs, symbols, and synchronicities evoked within *There Are No Coincidences* emitted different frequencies based on their position. For instance, I observed that the symbolism of the Geometry card was more clearly articulated when flanked by the Music and Numbers cards as opposed to the Delays and Dice cards. Because each arrangement generated a unique narrative, every single card's place within the deck was carefully considered. My goal, of course, was to amplify the meaning of each individual card within its respective category. So, after exploring a variety of options, I eventually found the sequence——the one you're interacting with today——that best expressed the cards' purest intentions.

Likewise, the cards' numbers——based on their intuitively guided organization——offer another mystical reference point. Perhaps certain numbers will indicate important dates or times? Addresses? Battery percentages? Highway exits? Your ability to interpret, analyze, and cultivate connections with the cards is informed by your inspiration; if you are receptive to their messages, the card's unique numbers will be sure to unlock even more possibilities.

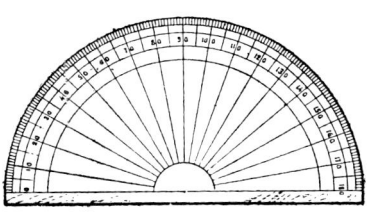

THERE ARE NO COINCIDENCES · 9

TANC

There Are No Coincidences is an immersive experience. This deck is the manifestation of profound metaphysical truths that transcend the cards themselves. Likewise, these cards are intended to underscore, emphasize, and amplify the signs, symbols, and synchronicities already illuminating your consciousness. Within the guidebook, I've included five examples of how each card's mystical presence might appear in your everyday life. Through this lens, we can explore the ubiquity of this phenomenon——in the world of TANC, nothing is casual. Everything has value, meaning, and significance. Accordingly, the TANCs embedded into each card reflect the infinite feedback loop between your day-to-day realities and the spiritual realm.

You may realize that you're already aligned with some of the TANC examples reflected in this guidebook. For instance, perhaps you had a special connection to a doorway in your childhood home, and identifying the association between doorways and Portals enables you to cultivate a richer understanding of its presence in your life. Alternatively, perhaps there were certain symbols that weren't as clearly defined, and the correspondences established within this deck will enable you to cultivate meaningful alignments between the physical and spiritual realms.

Note that the five TANC examples included in this guidebook will only begin to scratch the surface. Just as the keywords associated with each card are intended to enrich, elucidate, and inspire, each card's TANCs should springboard deeper spiritual cognition. There are countless ways and——truly——no limits to how signs, symbols, and synchronicities manifest in your reality, which is why calibrating your awareness is such an integral component of spiritual actualization. So, whether you're already well-versed in the language of correspondences or are just beginning to establish an allegorical vocabulary, TANCs will empower you to take your practice to the next level.

USING THE * CARDS

TANC IS A LANGUAGE. It's a way of tracing, tracking, and defining the magickal, electrical current that ignites existence on an individual and collective level. (Throughout the guidebook, I'll reference *magick* with a "ck," linking it to enchanted practices, as opposed to *magic* with a "c," which connotes tricks and illusions.) Likewise, this deck is designed to help strengthen your relationship with signs, symbols, and synchronicities. You may use these cards to provide insight into your current path——each will invite you to tune into a particular pattern or frequency, enabling you to determine whether you're moving in the right direction or if it's best to change course. Or, if you're feeling indecisive, you may use the cards for guidance: Each card will inspire new thoughts, perspective, and understanding for past, present, and future dynamics. These cards may also be used as a tool for divination. Perhaps you're interested in connecting with an ancestor or guide——these cards can serve as a conductor, enabling you to commune with spirits on the other side.

There are limitless ways to work with your deck, but here are a few recommendations to get you started:

SHUFFLING

While some people are extremely dexterous when handling cards, you certainly don't need to be a card dealer at a casino to successfully shuffle this deck (or any metaphysical deck, for that matter). Whether you choose to split the deck in half, using your thumbs to combine the piles, or prefer scattering the cards across a surface and scrambling them with the palms of your hands, your intention is the most important part of shuffling.

Your relationship with the deck is built on trust, honesty, and——most important——communication. Likewise, imagine the shuffling process like opening a new dialogue. The dynamic should be a back-and-forth, which

THERE ARE NO COINCIDENCES

means you're not relying exclusively on the deck to carry the conversation; you're participating as well. Indeed, you fortify your role in this exchange as you shuffle, so before you pull any cards, take a moment to connect with intention.

- *What do I want to discuss with the deck?*
- *What do I want to learn?*
- *What insight would help me navigate my current situation?*

When your intention is strong and the deck feels sufficiently shuffled, it's time to pull cards. The result of these pulls is often referred to as a "spread." There is no right or wrong way to work with spreads, but I've found that the most successful spreads are informed by the intent.

ONE-CARD

GUIDANCE

Pulling a single card will offer incredible depth, insight, and guidance. You may choose to lead with a question. I recommend closing your eyes and taking a moment to find the best wording for your query (for example, "What should I pay attention to right now?" or "What's the best path forward?") before dividing the deck in three sections. Use your intuition to stack the deck back together and pull the first card at the top of the pile. You may also incorporate a single card pull into your morning, afternoon, or evening routine, which will allow you to ritualize this expression, enabling you to experience the magick of that card within a twenty-four-hour cycle. Through this process, you'll develop unique relationships with each TANC. This consistent practice will offer guidance on how to move through your day, metabolize your current circumstances, or shed light on the best path forward.

THREE-CARD

NARRATIVE

To explore the narrative of a situation, consider working with a three-card spread. *Before* pulling the cards, assign meaning to each position—such as "past, present, future," "mind, body, spirit," "self, other, outcome," "internal, external, integration," or any other grouping of three that makes sense for your circumstances—so you know specifically what each card signifies. Once you've pulled the cards and assembled your spread, notice how the cards interact with each other. Is there any symmetry, repetition, harmony? Alternatively, you may observe contradictions, discrepancies, or dissonance—that's fine, too. After all, there are no coincidences; perhaps the disparity is a visual manifestation of a complex situation? The three-card spread allows each card to function individually, as well as within its broader sequence, so take your time exploring the incredible nuance when working with this formation.

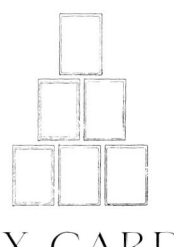

SIX-CARD

INVESTIGATION

Exploring the deck through a six-card spread offers comprehensive insight. When working with this ornate spread, consider what each position signifies *before* pulling the card, so there's a clear cohesion between the placement and its meaning. My suggestion is to allocate three cards to reflect your existing circumstances (cards one, two, and three), the tools you will need to employ moving forward (cards four and five), and the divine opportunity that awaits (card six). This is an excellent spread for navigating monumental transitions, transgressions, and transformations.

Remember that the deck wants to clarify, not confuse. And, because understanding the symbolism of each card requires interpretation, complicated spreads involving multiple cards can often muddle the message: It's hard to make sense of the signs, symbols, and synchronicities when the storyline becomes too convoluted. Developing a connection with each of the forty-four cards will take practice, patience, and focus, so don't

THERE ARE NO COINCIDENCES · 13

rush the process. Likewise, my recommendation for beginners is to pull fewer but interpret deeper. Display your card pull on an altar or at your writing desk——write about it in your journal, contemplate it in the shower, reflect on it during a walk. TANC lives within and without the boundaries of this container——that is, in fact, the essence of this practice.

REVERSALS

It is safe to say that, in the metaphysical realm, the moral binary of "good" and "bad" ceases to exist. Everything is complex. Everything is layered. Everything is an amorphous, iridescent mass of pleasure and pain, success and failure, love and loss. Likewise, every card in this deck is embedded with multiples, containing both auspicious, positive attributes, as well as tests, challenges, and cautionary tales. When working with the deck, I recommend noting your immediate, visceral reaction to a card (What is its energetic vibration? How does it make you feel? What memories does it conjure?), and then give yourself time and space——perhaps through inhales and exhales, or within the pages of a designated journal——to broaden your interpretation. Are there other, perhaps less straightforward, implications that add dimensionality to your initial analysis? When you expand your vantage, what unexpected nuances are revealed in this sign, symbol, or synchronicity? How does this card push back on, defy, or resist the obvious associations? Mysticism demands fluidity, poetry, and subversion, so don't be surprised if a card appears to shape-shift, with new meanings and connotations unfolding over time. Sometimes the cards will pose more questions than answers——that's part of the magick.

This is a long-winded way of addressing reversals. For those unfamiliar with this term, reversals refer to a distinctive interpretation of the card when it appears upside down. Traditionally, reversals are approached as opposites; in other words, whatever the card means and signifies is——quite literally——flipped on its head in a 180 degree turn. Many tarot readers, soothsayers, and divinators use reversals. Many others——present company included——do not. Accordingly, my intention was to pack each sign, symbol, and synchronicity with so much depth, dimensionality, and nuance that multiple truths exist whether the card is upright, reversed, or spun around like a Hanukkah dreidel. No matter how you look at the card, it should *always* contain a 360 degree experience. If you, however, feel compelled to work with reversals, go right ahead. The cards——like your practice and the Moon and all expressions of illumination——are intended to wax and wane. So go ahead and experiment, discover, and explore. At the end of the day, your deck is an extension of your consciousness, animated *exclusively* by your magick. You will always know best.

INTERPRETATING THE * CARDS

TANC DEMANDS INTERPRETATION. But that's the tricky thing about this material—no singular explanation could possibly cover the expanse of meaning, as well as the specific nuances of its significance on a personal level. In this realm, harmony coexists with contradiction—we're in a liminal space now, so make yourself at home.

But before you drift into the abyss of metaphors and allegory, let's clarify this deck's most fundamental anchor: There's nothing more important than your personal relationship with each card. As we've discussed, TANC is a manifestation of consciousness, so your individual connection to signs, symbols, and synchronicities will ignite this deck with intention, mysticism, and meaning. To fortify your bond with TANC, I recommend exploring the materiality of the cards as physical objects, as well as reading the comprehensive analyses presented in this guidebook.

You'll discover that the style of my interpretation varies from card to card, ranging from mathematic to historic, mythologic to anecdotal. The reason for this is twofold: One, because I wanted to introduce readers to a range of interpretation techniques, and two, because that's the way I personally approach interpretation—an amalgam of fact, fiction, stoicism, and poetry. TANC is electrified by creativity, mystery, and imagination.

Likewise, as you personalize the deck, I invite you to experiment with interpretations. Here are some questions to consider:

- *What was my initial impression of this card?*
- *Has this sign, symbol, or synchronicity previously appeared in my life? If so, in which way(s)?*
- *How do I connect with the guidebook's interpretation?*
- *What does this card mean in the context of my current reality?*
- *Why would this card appear right now?*

THERE ARE NO COINCIDENCES

CATEGORY

COSMOS

THE ELEVEN CARDS INCLUDED in the Cosmos category are linked to astrology, astronomy, and celestial mythology. They illuminate signs, symbols, and synchronicities that relate to planetary orbits, space travel, and/or extraterrestrial discoveries, as well as spiritual, poetic interpretations of stars, planets, and celestial bodies. Exploring your birth chart (that is, a map of the sky based on the date, time, and location of your birth), as well as horoscopes and transits (the movement of the planets in real time) will deepen your relationship with this category.

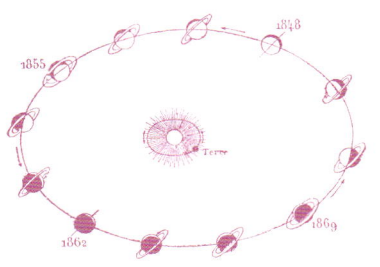

EXAMPLE: The Saturn card speaks to restrictions, responsibilities, and time. As you explore how these concepts appear in your life, consider researching the position of Saturn in your birth chart to learn more about this astrological placement on a personal level.

THERE ARE NO COINCIDENCES · 17

COSMOS

1.
THE ASCENDANT

COSMOS

2.
THE SUN

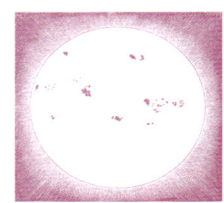

COSMOS

5.
VENUS

COSMOS

6.
MARS

COSMOS

3.
THE MOON

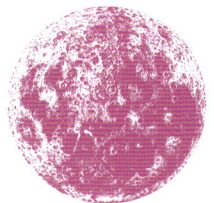

COSMOS

4.
MERCURY

COSMOS

7.
JUPITER

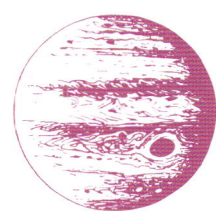

COSMOS

8.
SATURN

COSMOS

9.

URANUS

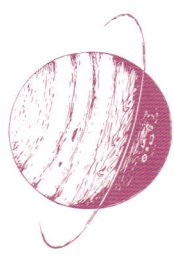

COSMOS

10.

NEPTUNE

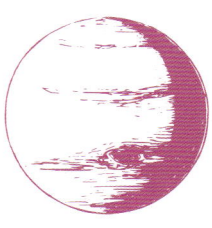

COSMOS

11.

PLUTO

CARD 1. THE ASCENDANT   CATEGORY COSMOS

KEYWORDS

❧

Perspective
Narrative
Reputation
Origins

❧

TANC

❧

Landscapes
Symmetry
Eyeglasses
Highways
Patterns

❧

PERSONAL NOTES

❧ **STORY** ❧

IN ASTROLOGY, THE ASCENDANT——also referred to as the Rising Sign——depicts the area of the zodiac that was coming up over the eastern horizon at your exact moment of birth. When it comes to the Ascendant, the exact time is a critical detail; this sensitive point changes zodiac signs every two hours and a degree every four minutes. Although most people identify astrology with their Sun (that is, the position the Sun occupied on the day of birth), prior to the advent of magazine horoscopes in the early twentieth century, the Ascendant was the entry point for astrological analysis——and with good reason. The Ascendant establishes the architecture for your entire birth chart, as well as the themes, patterns, and cycles that continue to surface throughout your lifetime. The Ascendant reveals your mission. Your perspective. Your physical realities as you navigate your day-to-day experiences, as well as your philosophical vantage when you tilt your head up toward the stars. The Ascendant is your inimitable experience on this planet——it's your story.

❧ **INTERPRETATION** ❧

The Ascendant asks you to explore your unique point of view. Perhaps you're approaching a new situation with an old attitude? Or maybe you're hoping to shift the outcome of a familiar tale? Whatever circumstances you're currently facing, the Ascendant encourages you to explore them within the broader context of your lived experience. The Ascendant is a reminder that no two people see the world through the same set of eyes and, accordingly, your impression of your joys, disappointments, hopes, and sorrows is part of the ongoing themes that comprise your narrative. What's more, remember that while certain aspects of your perspective may be static, you can adjust your footing. Approaching your situation from a slightly shifted angle may invite an entirely different interpretation . . . and maybe it's as simple as the recognition of repetition. Set your timer for four minutes——the time it takes the Ascendant to shift one degree——and, within that short duration, challenge yourself to adopt a new outlook. There's a reason you're here, experiencing life exactly as you are——the Ascendant invites you to find that distinctive theme that defines your journey.

THERE ARE NO COINCIDENCES   ·   21

CARD 2. THE SUN   **CATEGORY** COSMOS

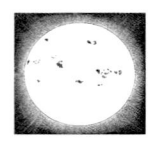

KEYWORDS
❖
Illumination
Joy
Ego
Vitality
❖

TANC
❖
Daytime
Crowns
Sunflowers
Gold
The Heart
The Zodiac
Sign *of* Leo
❖

PERSONAL NOTES

❖ **STORY** ❖

THE SUN NEEDS NO INTRODUCTION. The epicenter of our solar system, the Sun is so spectacular—so ineffably divine—that its self-generated energy is the origin of everything. We may observe how all living organisms instinctively turn their faces sunward, mirroring the planets' own urge to drift toward this radiant star. Suffice it to say, the Sun surely knows how to attract attention. To worship the Sun—whether by lying poolside on a hot summer day or venerating solar deities through seasonal ceremonies—is to honor the electrical current that animates existence. The Sun's power is incomparable ... but that doesn't always mean it's kind. Just as prolonged exposure to the Sun burns the skin and boils the mind, malevolent rulers adopt solar imagery to impose unchecked authority. Thankfully, the cosmos has a solution to this as well: Each day, we look to the west as the Sun dips over the horizon, marking a time of humility, release, and perspective. As the bright star dips beneath our eyeline, temperatures drop, shadows expand, and energy wanes. In this steady, earnest twenty-four-hour cycle, we can experience an entire life, death, and rebirth as orchestrated by the Sun.

❖ **INTERPRETATION** ❖

When the Sun shows up, it's time to check in with yourself. What are you doing? Why are you doing it? And, perhaps most important, is it making you happy? To keep up with the Sun's extraordinary exuberance, you need to tap into your own energetic centers—that innate essence of vitality that electrifies your spirit. The presence of the Sun asks you to consider what the concept of "life force" means to you, ensuring that the exhaustion of day-to-day responsibilities hasn't eclipsed your solar power. Additionally, this card serves as a reminder that you have the strength, dynamism, and determination to accomplish whatever you've set out to achieve—just make sure you're not coming in too hot! While your abilities are remarkable, the presence of the Sun asks that your motivation is coming from true, heart-led passions as opposed to ego or pomposity. Remember, the magick of the Sun is that it simply *is*. Likewise, you don't need to prove your worth; simply radiate your truth and the opportunities will follow.

CARD 3. THE MOON   CATEGORY COSMOS

KEYWORDS

❖

Compassion
Nourishment
Privacy
Sensitivity

❖

TANC

❖

Nighttime
Crescents
Fearls
Silver
The Zodiac
Sign *of* Cancer

❖

PERSONAL NOTES

❖ STORY ❖

ALTHOUGH WE LIVE IN A SOLAR WORLD——calendars correspond with the Sun's daily performance——the Moon offers a totally different perspective. A consistent shape-shifter, the Moon glides through its own twenty-eight-day orbit, defined through its dramatic undulation against the backdrop of darkness. The cycle begins with a New Moon, with the celestial satellite hidden among the stars. There is no nocturnal illumination and, likewise, this is considered the time to plant seeds, set intentions, and prepare for the Moon's tremendous swell. As the Moon transitions into its waxing phase, it begins it sensual revelation, animating the psyche through its emergence. The culmination of this awareness is defined by the Full Moon——the dynamic phase of total and complete visibility. The Full Moon, displaying maximum exposure, transforms ordinary objects into mysterious entities of light and shadows, mirrors of the Moon itself. Almost instantaneously, the Moon decides you've seen enough and prepares its descent——the waning phases——back into the darkness, pulling the ocean's inky tides along for the ride.

❖ INTERPRETATION ❖

The presence of this card invites you to explore your own emotional ebb and flow. Your internal experience is never static: Like the Moon, it's a reflection of your daily circumstances and conditions. So, how do you *feel*? When you drop inward, what does your psyche——your dreams, your subconscious, your private narrative——have to say? Sometimes these truths must be presented publicly, just as the magnanimous Full Moon demands attention. But, other times, these discoveries are private and personal, and awareness of these complex emotional experiences is best processed intimately. Regardless of how you choose to express your inner world, remember that——even when the Moon isn't visible——our psychological experience is ever-present. To honor the Moon is to recognize its incredible impact on virtually every aspect of our lives. Embrace the fluctuation.

THERE ARE NO COINCIDENCES · 23

CARD 4. MERCURY   CATEGORY COSMOS

KEYWORDS

❖

Communication
Contemplation
Discourse
Logic

❖

TANC

❖

Messages
Calendars
Transportation
Journals
The Zodiac
Signs *of*
Gemini *and*
Virgo

❖

PERSONAL NOTES

❖ **STORY** ❖

MERCURY IS THE CLOSEST PLANET to the sun, and the smallest of the rocky planets in the asteroid belt. Mercury whips around the sun——completing an orbit in only eighty-eight days——and, from our perspective on Earth, the planet appears to move backward three or four times each year, creating an optical illusion known as "Mercury Retrograde." Although all planets (excluding the Luminaries——the Sun and Moon) have retrograde orbits, Mercury's is certainly the most notorious. In classical antiquity, Roman Mercury was the divine messenger, representing merchants, travelers, transporters, and even thieves (his lore was derived from the Greek deity, Hermes). Likewise, Mercury is associated with communication, expression, language, and matters of the mind—— so it should be no surprise that problems arise when things go backwards. In mythology, Mercury is often depicted sporting a winged helmet or sandals, wearing a satchel, and/or carrying a wand entwined by two snakes, referred to as his "caduceus." Mercury's caduceus was used to guide the deceased into Pluto's underworld or——for those who were mistakenly escorted——bring the dead back to life (this mystical property is why the caduceus also represents health and medicine and is often seen on hospitals and ambulances). Applied on a daily basis, Mercury's greatest strengths are expressed through the power of words.

❖ **INTERPRETATION** ❖

This card implores you to consider the impact of expression. Thoughts, feelings, sensitivities——even dreams, goals, and ambitions——can function independently from our articulation, so the presence of Mercury invites you to focus exclusively on the transmission. Are you really saying what you mean? Is there a disconnect between what you want and what you're expressing? Perhaps you've been indirect, padding your intentions with fillers like niceties, question words, or qualifications. If so, Mercury's presence urges you to be more straightforward: Be clear, honest, and matter-of-fact. Or maybe your current situation requires a bit more finesse: How can your dialogue be more lyrical? Persuasive? Working with Mercury is recognizing the incredible alchemy of communication——by using the right messaging, even the most stressful challenges can transform into monumental opportunities in the blink of an eye. This is true magick.

CARD 5. VENUS   CATEGORY COSMOS

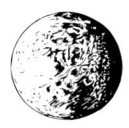

KEYWORDS

❧

Romance
Adoration
Infatuation
Pleasure

❧

TANC

❧

Perfume
Pastries
Rose Petals
The Zodiac
Signs *of* Taurus
and Libra

❧

PERSONAL NOTES

❧ **STORY** ❧

WHEN COMPARED TO PLANET EARTH, Venus is similar in size, mass, density, and even gravity. But Venus is the hottest planet in the solar system: Its thick, dense sulfuric atmosphere traps heat, causing surface temperatures rise to 880 degrees F (471 degrees C) and creating a sweltering inferno. For some, Venus's monstrous conditions might come as a bit of a surprise——from our vantage on Earth, this illuminated celestial body sure looks beautiful. It is, in fact, the brightest planet in the sky. This astronomical exploration of Venus is TANC, perfectly mirroring its origin story in Greco-Roman mythology: When Uranus, the primordial sky god, became a power-hungry tyrant, his son——Saturn——used a scythe to castrate him and tossed Uranus's genitals into the ocean. And, from the debris of organs and blood and semen, a viscous foam began to form, ultimately transforming into Venus, the goddess of love, wealth, and fertility (Venus is the Roman equivalent of the Greek deity Aphrodite). Indeed, Venus's archetype reflects the paradoxes of romanization. In astrology, Venus reveals our idealized version of love. Venus symbolizes our perception of beauty, as well as what others find magnetic about your character. While these desires might not always be sustainable (let alone realistic), Venus reminds us that life isn't always about our needs——sometimes our *wants* are just as important.

❧ **INTERPRETATION** ❧

When the Venus card shows up, consider your relationship with desire. Although love and sex coexist, the energy of Venus isn't specifically carnal (lust is expressed through Mars, the planet of action); Venus's urges surround beauty, opulence, courtship, and even aesthetics. Unchecked, Venusian energy can certainly manifest through superficiality or materialism——perhaps the presence of this card implores you to consider the role vanity is playing in your current circumstances. Might your *idealized* version of a dynamic be clouding your ability to accept the truth? Alternatively, this card's presence may encourage you to prioritize your Venusian sensibilities. Maybe you've skewed too heavily toward logic, pragmatism, and responsibility and Venus's appearance in this deck serves as a reminder that life is more than utility bills. Pleasure is paramount.

THERE ARE NO COINCIDENCES

CARD 6. MARS   CATEGORY COSMOS

KEYWORDS

❖

Determination
Tenacity
Lust
Drive

❖

TANC

❖

Trophies
Sports Cars
Vibrators
Steel
The Zodiac
Signs *of* Aries
and Scorpio

❖

PERSONAL NOTES

❖ STORY ❖

IS THERE LIFE ON MARS? Humans have been fascinated by this elusive red planet for thousands of years, but it is only in the last few centuries that technology has enabled a deeper expression of these curiosities: Missions to Mars have captivated our attention in science, literature, entertainment, and even politics. And——in the perfect poeticism that is TANC——our determination to understand this celestial neighbor is a beautiful expression of Mars's symbolic archetype. Although Ares, the god of war in ancient Greece, was depicted as violent and reckless, Mars——the Roman counterpart——was a bit more dignified. Mars governed military conquests, battles, and soldiers, as well as agricultural innovation and farmers. Mars is forceful, ambitious, and purposeful; in astrology, Mars in our birth chart reveals the way we find motivation, take action, and get things done. Moreover, since the transition from cold to warm weather precipitates action, energy, and vitality, Mars is connected to the spring equinox . . . and the corresponding copulation of the birds and bees. Mars governs all matters of the thrust, and is associated with virility, carnality, and lust. On a physiological level, we experience Mars energy through our pounding heart and pumping blood——this is, indeed, the essence of life on Mars.

❖ INTERPRETATION ❖

Do you *really* want it? Prove it. In quintessential Martian fashion, this card will often appear in the form of a challenge. Mars is about dynamism, vigor, and motion——so, if you've been sitting around feeling sorry for yourself, the appearance of this card invites you to push past the drudgery. What steps can you take, right now, to get closer to your goal? How can you harness that powerful, innate vitality that burns brightly within the depths of your soul; the magnetism that defines your unique will, determination, and drive? Can you dial it up, even if only just a few small notches? Perhaps the answer is no. Maybe you've already reached capacity and the presence of this card reflects exactly how hard you've been fighting. If you've been burning the candle at both ends, the Mars card may reflect your sheer exhaustion. Whether you're applying or retracting, this card speaks to your innate force. It's time to take action.

CARD 7. JUPITER   CATEGORY COSMOS

KEYWORDS

❦

Luck
Opportunity
Indulgence
Optimism

❦

TANC

❦

Casinos
Libraries
Tickets
Temples
The Zodiac
Signs *of*
Sagittarius *and*
Pisces

❦

PERSONAL NOTES

❦ **STORY** ❦

IS BIGGER *REALLY* BETTER? When it comes to Jupiter, all signs point to yes. The largest planet in our solar system, Jupiter plays a major role in our day-to-day lives——in fact, we wouldn't be here without this massive gas giant. Jupiter's enormous size (it's approximately 318 times larger than Earth) exudes a monumental gravitational pull that prevents millions of asteroids from careening toward the Sun. Frozen in space and time, this debris remains suspended between Mars and Jupiter, creating a dense band of rocks known as the asteroid belt. Jupiter's benevolent magnetism is high stakes . . . and that's just the way Jupiter likes it. Jupiter—— also known as its Greek counterpart, Zeus—— was the king of the gods in Roman mythology. The planet of expansion, Jupiter is associated with luck, fortune, and fate. Jupiter recognizes the relationship between risk and reward, and likewise, this archetype is willing to put some skin in the game. Whether it's posting up at the casino, booking an international flight to study an esoteric philosophy at a remote destination, or making a massive down payment on a sizable investment property, Jupiter's motto is always "go big or go home."

❦ **INTERPRETATION** ❦

Jupiter's presence can be extremely auspicious: Perhaps there's a new opportunity coming your way. Or, if you've been feeling listless and uninspired, Jupiter's appearance may signify a brilliant eureka moment that enables you to look at your situation from a totally different point of view. Jupiter's expansive scope enables us to broaden our horizons, and likewise, the appearance of this card indicates great potential. But be careful: Jupiter knows *nothing* of moderation, so this card could also signal that certain behaviors, ideas, or compulsions have gotten out of hand. As such a massive planet, Jupiter's all about scale: Jupiter magnifies anything it touches, which means that whatever circumstances you're currently navigating have been expanded exponentially——maybe even blown out of proportion. In this case, the Jupiter card may come as a warning: When in doubt, slow down. At the end of the day, there's nothing more sustainable than moderation.

CARD **8. SATURN**   CATEGORY COSMOS

KEYWORDS

❖

Commitment
Responsibility
Restriction
Wisdom

❖

TANC

❖

Wrinkles
Rakes
Clocks
Contracts
The Zodiac
Signs *of*
Capricorn *and*
Aquarius

❖

**PERSONAL
NOTES**

❖ **STORY** ❖

SATURN MAY NOT BE THE LARGEST PLANET in the solar system——but it is the most stabilizing. In fact, Saturn's immense gravitational pull tugs on Jupiter, preventing it from hurtling toward the Sun (and destroying Earth along the way). Distant and elusive, Saturn's existence maintains cosmic equilibrium, holding all other celestial bodies in place to ensure long-term sustainability. And with both the astronomy and astrology intertwined in perfect TANC harmony, it should come as no surprise that Saturn is the essence of boundaries, restriction, and responsibility. In mythology, Saturn is associated with Chronos——the personification of time. Saturn's orbit is one of the most notorious milestones in astrology: The Saturn Return occurs approximately every twenty-nine years, when Saturn concludes its long journey around the Sun. During our Saturn Return, we become keenly aware that it is our sole responsibility to actualize our potential . . . and that the clock is ticking. Indeed, Saturn's symbolism teaches us powerful lessons about hard work, accountability, and——perhaps most important——the gift of the present moment.

❖ **INTERPRETATION** ❖

Oh, were you planning on taking a shortcut? Saturn begs to differ. When this card emerges, it's time to get serious. In this deck, the Saturn card symbolizes maturity, responsibility, and commitment; forget whining, complaining, or feeling sorry for yourself——Saturn's tough-love approach says, "It is what it is." Does that seem a bit harsh? That's the whole point! From a symbolic perspective, Saturn's function is cold stoicism: Saturn asks you to look at the reality of your situation——no matter how disappointing or frustrating it may be——and accept it at face value, acknowledging all the thorns and blemishes and failures. Life isn't easy . . . but now what? Baked within Saturn's severe angles are themes of patience, wisdom, and genuine achievement. Yes, in order to create something that is *truly* built to last, you will need to overcome impossible odds——but, right now, the presence of Saturn is a green light from the universe. So long as you're willing to put in the work, you absolutely have what it takes to reap the most fulfilling rewards.

CARD 9. URANUS   CATEGORY COSMOS

KEYWORDS

❖

Revolution
Innovation
Shock
Brilliance

❖

TANC

❖

Lightning
Earthquakes
Social Media
Tattoos
The Zodiac
Sign *of*
Aquarius

❖

PERSONAL NOTES

❖ STORY ❖

URANUS IS A REAL WEIRDO——and not just because it's the butt of all jokes. Uranus was the first planet spotted through a telescope, a monumental scientific breakthrough that corresponded with the technological advancements of the eighteenth century. Additionally, Uranus is the only planet named after a Greek god (as opposed to a Roman deity), and it's tilted so far on its axis——a stunning 97.77 degrees——that it essentially orbits sideways. These eccentric features perfectly mirror its symbolic significance: From an astrological perspective, Uranus represents technology, rebellion, innovation, and raw genius. Frozen and distant, Uranus isn't concerned with day-to-day tasks and responsibilities—— Uranian energy ideates on a big-picture, long-term, macro scale. Detached and unemotional, Uranus's motto is "Hey, it's nothing personal." Indeed, this revolutionary planet rejects conformity at all costs: Free-thinking and unconventional, Uranus will always choose chaos over structure. Although Uranian energy can skew toward destruction (in certain branches of astrology, Uranus is associated with natural disasters such as earthquakes and tornados), Uranus's core motivation is progress. Fundamentally, Uranus is looking toward the future.

❖ INTERPRETATION ❖

When you encounter Uranus in this deck, consider taking a step back. And then another one. And another. Just like the ice giant at the edge of our solar system, you're going to need perspective. Uranus demands a bird's-eye view, and likewise, the Uranus card in this deck indicates the need to broaden your vantage point as a way of propelling radical change. Perhaps you're a bit stuck, stifled——maybe even bored? The same old routines and schedules and conversations are making you feel trapped. Fortunately, Uranus serves as a reminder that, in an instant, everything can change. Likewise, Uranus's presence may indicate that a massive, cataclysmic shift is on the horizon——brace yourself for a major upheaval. Alternatively, the Uranus card may also suggest that, in order to tap into your brilliance, you need to step outside your comfort zone and shake things up. Sure, you may ruffle some feathers, but you know what they say: Well-behaved people rarely make history. Don't be afraid to stir the pot.

THERE ARE NO COINCIDENCES

CARD 10. NEPTUNE   CATEGORY COSMOS

KEYWORDS

❖

Illusion
Eeception
Escape
Fantasy

❖

TANC

❖

Vapor
Poetry
Pills
Mermaids
The Zodiac
Sign *of* Pisces

❖

**PERSONAL
NOTES**

❖ STORY ❖

OVER 2.7 BILLION MILES FROM THE SUN, Neptune's landscape is truly otherworldly. Neptune does not have a solid surface, but rather a thick atmosphere (believed to be hydrogen, helium, and methane) that encapsulates a scalding stew of "icy" materials (water, methane, ammonia)——bizarre, contradictory conditions that perfectly align with our astrological interpretation of the celestial body: Neptune symbolizes illusion, delusion, and psychic depth. In fact, Neptune's existence was predicted before it was even discovered, deepening this planet's eerie connection between fantasy and reality. Named after the Roman sea god (with Poseidon as the Greek counterpart), Neptune reigns over a subterranean kingdom, where everything is submerged in water and nothing is quite as it seems. Neptune governs dreams, psychic powers, and creative pursuits, with an emphasis on photography, film, and entertainment. Themes of glamour and celebrity are baked into Neptune's enchanting magick——but fame can come at a cost. Neptune's dense fog is also associated with idealization, confusion, escapism, addiction, and self-destruction. Though Neptune's beguiling mist can transport us into other dimensions——enabling us to transcend the humdrum of normalcy——we must anchor ourselves firmly in truth, otherwise reality can become as ephemeral as smoke and mirrors.

❖ INTERPRETATION ❖

When Neptune appears, you're encouraged to dive into the wells of your creative spirit, extracting powerful expressions of art, music, and poetry. Neptune speaks to the subconscious, visions, and innate mysticism——this card invites you to become your own muse. What would it take for you to live the life you've relegated to fantasy? Who would you have to become? This card asks you to chart the distance between your current reality and your wildest dreams. But there's a fine line between perception and deception——likewise, this card may also issue a warning. Perhaps you're getting lost in romantic idealization? Or maybe you're avoiding painful realities by drifting into escapist tendencies; Neptune may reflect the use of substances or addictive behavior. Remember, Neptune is the intersection of the physical and astral realms——if you find yourself drifting too far into the latter, be sure to find your footing.

CARD 11. PLUTO   CATEGORY COSMOS

KEYWORDS

❖

Transformation
Upheaval
Intensity
Rebirth

❖

TANC

❖

Oil
Vermin
Liquidation
Diamonds
The Zodiac
Sign *of* Pisces

❖

PERSONAL NOTES

❖ **STORY** ❖

IN 1930, SCIENTISTS DISCOVERED a small, rocky celestial body located approximately 3.9 billion miles from the Sun. Impossibly distant and fascinatingly tiny, this celestial body was named Pluto, taking the name of the Roman god of the underworld (with Hades as the Greek counterpart). Although Pluto's title as the ninth planet in our solar system has since been revoked (Pluto became classified as a "dwarf planet" in 2006), its significance in the astrological community remains profound. Like its mythological namesake, Pluto is believed to govern secrets, clandestine information, and the monumental metaphoremes experienced over a lifetime. Intensely powerful, Pluto drills into the core, unearthing truths buried deep beneath the surface. Accessing these subterranean domains is no small feat——likewise, Pluto's realm includes death, sex, and occultism. This beguiling celestial body can navigate even the most complex networks, quietly tearing apart systems from the inside out. Pluto isn't afraid of demolition . . . but there's a method to the madness. Closely associated with the Phoenix——the mythological bird who rises from the ashes——Pluto invites us to explore the limitless possibilities of renewal and rebirth. Indeed, the best way to navigate Plutonian energy is through surrender.

❖ **INTERPRETATION** ❖

Pluto signals cataclysmic transformation. Perhaps its presence reflects your current circumstances: You've already begun dismantling the infrastructure, and this card mirrors the profundity of this life-changing experience. After all, Pluto is neither an ending nor a beginning; it's a process. Alternatively, this card may surface when you need to go deeper. Perhaps you've been clinging to an existing status quo, afraid of what you'll discover. It's important to remember, however, that averting your eyes is not the same as repairing the damage——if something is broken, it will remain that way until it is fixed. Pluto invites you to take a deep breath and descend into the basement. Sure, it may not be pretty——musty cellars are filled with bulky equipment and unsightly storage—— but those machines and control panels and levers are the heartbeat of the home. And maintenance is mandatory. With Pluto on your side, you're armed with strategy, courage, and the magick of regeneration. Don't be afraid to flip the switch.

THERE ARE NO COINCIDENCES

CATEGORY

NATURE

CARDS

12
~
22

THE NATURE CATEGORY contains signs, symbols, and synchronicities of organic matter, including elements, plants, animals, weather, and raw materials. The cards included in this section may be animated through outdoor activities, environmental conditions, and/or day-to-day experiences with flora and fauna. This category——and the cards it contains——also fortifies a connection to the spiritual essence of "Mother Earth" that exists cross-culturally, as articulated through a variety of names, mythologies, and narratives. The category invites a deeper awareness and sensitivity of other species and entities who cohabitate on this planet.

EXAMPLE: The Birds card is associated with messages, guidance, and trust. These concepts exist independently from the species, but will be amplified if or when you encounter a bird (or the presence of a bird, such as a feather or nest) as you move throughout your day.

THERE ARE NO COINCIDENCES · 33

NATURE

12.

FIRE

NATURE

13.

EARTH

NATURE

16.

TREES

NATURE

17.

FLOWERS

NATURE

14.

AIR

NATURE

15.

WATER

NATURE

18.

INSECTS

NATURE

19.

BIRDS

NATURE
20.
ANIMALS

NATURE
21.
FOG

NATURE
22.
STONES

CARD 12. FIRE   CATEGORY NATURE

KEYWORDS

❖

Passion
Vigor
Momentum
Recklessness

❖

TANC

❖

Candles
Matches
Fireplaces
Stovetops
The Zodiac
Signs *of* Aries,
Leo, *and*
Sagittarius

❖

PERSONAL NOTES

❖ STORY ❖

FIRE IS A FORCE OF SPIRIT, ANIMATION, and dynamism. Mythology links the birth of consciousness to fire-making; our ability to create, control, and manage flame defines our humanity. Fire offers light, warmth, and protection; it detoxifies and purifies food, ignites machinery, and enables vision in even the darkest nights. This naturally electric element embodies provocative potentiality——it sparks artistic creation, scientific invention, and even revolutionary activism. But fire is inherently wild. Fire ripples across landscapes with tremendous force, instantaneously transforming bucolic pastures into smoldering infernos. Scorching heat, suffocating ash, and noxious smoke are byproducts of fire's unparalleled fury. But from the fuming rubble emerges new possibilities: Life begins again.

❖ INTERPRETATION ❖

When this card emerges, take inventory of the flames in your life. Perhaps you're on the edge of a monumental breakthrough——if so, this card is an invitation to light the match for heart-led ignition. Kindle the flame, nurturing it from a tiny spark to a roaring, self-sustaining blaze. Alternatively, the presence of this card may signal a warning: Systems or circumstances have become insurmountable. Do you need to use the other elements——water, sand, carbon dioxide——to de-escalate the situation? Or perhaps it needs to burn. In times like these, the best solution is regeneration. Let it sizzle, smoke, and——ultimately——rise again. Fire is, after all, both the ending and beginning of all creation stories.

THERE ARE NO COINCIDENCES

CARD 13. EARTH   CATEGORY NATURE

KEYWORDS

❖

Stability
Materiality
Rigidity
Safety

❖

TANC

❖

Soil
Leaves
Wood
Mountains
The Zodiac
Signs *of*
Taurus, Virgo,
and Capricorn

❖

PERSONAL NOTES

❖ **STORY** ❖

IN ALCHEMICAL TRADITIONS, Earth is one of the four primary elements, representing all terrestrial, land-bound matter. Earth speaks to nature, especially the organic flora and fauna of this planet's diverse landscapes. It's the pine trees. It's the vineyards. It's the twisting, coiling ivy that snakes up an old lamppost. But, of course, these identifiable expressions of Earth exist aboveground——Earth also exists below, within the soil and roots and mycelium. While leaves stretch toward the Sun, tendrils expand beneath the surface, seeking subterranean nutrients and anchoring vegetation through sturdy engineering. Indeed, Earth is also represented in the form of inorganic structures, including material things, architectural structures, and currency. Earth manifests through the concept of having, which——if unregulated——can also manifest as hoarding. Earth reminds us that, within nature, nothing is ever really owned; it's only ever borrowed and repurposed. There's no distinction between the sprouting bud and the rotting leaf——all matter coexists harmoniously. Indeed, Earth represents stability, structure, and security within the practical, physical world.

❖ **INTERPRETATION** ❖

What do you *have*? What do you *want*? How will you get it? Metaphysical practices teach us to spark passion to ignite creativity, think abstractly to generate new ideas, and explore our deepest emotions to hone extrasensory intuition. But actually *integrating* these skills within daily life is a completely different story. No matter how skilled you may be at navigating the nonphysical astral realm——the domain of wishes and spirits and synchronicities——you are, for better or worse, a product of nature in need of nutrients and shelter and support. Likewise, the Earth card requires us to connect with the physical domain——food, resources, movement——to ensure that we are both present and firmly anchored. Alternatively, the presence of this card may also signal excess stubbornness, obstinance, or even greed. The Earth card compels you to drop your shoulders, unclench your jaw, and feel the ground beneath your feet. You're here. You're alive. Now, ask yourself again, what do you *really* need?

CARD 14. AIR   CATEGORY NATURE

KEYWORDS

❖

Thoughts
Networks
Nerves
Connections

❖

TANC

❖

Wi-Fi
Puzzles
Wind
Smog
The Zodiac
Signs *of*
Gemini, Libra,
and Aquarius

❖

PERSONAL NOTES

❖ **STORY** ❖

IN MANY ANCIENT CULTURES, air had a big responsibility: Air was the invisible buttress that dutifully separated earth from sky, propping up the heavens to ensure they didn't come crashing down on our mortal plane. What's more, this formless matter served as a conductor, passing messages back and forth between the realms: prayers, commands, punishments, blessings. Modern mysticism upholds this early mythology——air is the channel, the mediator, the conduit. Air enables us to transfer information from one place to another, swiftness that is expeditated through both gentle breezes and harsh gusts of wind. Quite literally, air is atmosphere: It's the stuff of evaporated, distilled, and vaporized solid matter——it's the invisible imprint of reality. Likewise, air is associated with the mind and how we process information, both interpersonally and intellectually. Air is cerebral, cognitive, and omniscient, and speaks to the way complex data is metabolized by thoughts, ideas, and belief systems. Unlike the other elements, the formless nature of air allows it to transcend circumstances. But static air can become noxious——a petri dish for viruses and containments and outdated ideologies. Indeed, there's a reason we're often instructed to "get some fresh air"——circulation is an integral component of understanding.

❖ **INTERPRETATION** ❖

The Air card inspires thought. When this card appears, take a moment to consider your point of view and the ways in which you express your ideas. Are you being fair, balanced, and open-minded? If so, the presence of the Air card may arrive as an affirmation, substantiating your ability to cultivate creative solutions to complicated circumstances. Your ability to rise above the chaos——breaking the situation into the smallest molecules—— will enable you to communicate your innate truths. Or perhaps you need some air. Whether you're cracking a window, stepping out for a brisk walk, or simply moving into a different room, the Air card may signal a need to make environmental changes. Fundamentally, air is ambiance, so if your conditions feel stifling or suffocating, the best solution may be a change in scenery.

THERE ARE NO COINCIDENCES   ·   39

CARD 15. WATER   CATEGORY NATURE

KEYWORDS

❖

Emotions
Deluge
Surrender
Clairvoyance

❖

TANC

❖

Rain
Faucets
Tears
Oceans
The Zodiac
Signs *of*
Cancer, Scorpio, *and* Pisces

❖

PERSONAL NOTES

❖ **STORY** ❖

WHETHER YOU'RE CURLING YOUR TOES AROUND A mossy rock, preparing to jump into a cool summer creek, or curled up in a fetal position, churning howls from the depth of your core, the question remains the same: "How deep is it?" Indeed, the link between water and psyche is so strong—so profoundly interconnected—the two might be tangible and intangible expressions of the same matter. Of course, just as there are different ways to explore emotion, water has myriad shapes and forms—including the contours of whatever vessel it occupies. There's the playful sensibility of the shore—the whimsical flutter of the tides as it rolls foam and bubbles and pebbles across the coastline. There's the insatiable thrust of rivers: powerful systems that pump life upstream and downstream, mirroring the motion of our own veins and arteries. And, of course, there are oceans—unmatched in might and mystery. Thousands of miles beneath the surface of the Earth, subterranean ecosystems thrive in high-pressure landscapes void of sunlight, heat, or air. Perhaps this, too, exists within each of us: incomprehensible truths that—every now and then—flow through us like waves.

❖ **INTERPRETATION** ❖

The Water card asks you to connect with your internal experience. Accepting the metaphysical axiom of "as above, so below," we can surmise that the deepest water also lives within our psyche. To describe the limitless subconscious domain that stores the entirety of your existence—every conversation you've ever had, every stranger you've ever passed, every disappointment you've ever embodied—is as utterly unfathomable as the deepest sea. Or the farthest planets. Or the meaning of life. Accordingly, the Water card invites you to step out of the logical, intellectual domain and flow into your extrasensory experiences. How do you *feel*? What do you *sense*? What is the *vibe*? The answers you seek exist within, so the appearance of this sublimely mystical card demands inward reflection. Yes, the intensity of your emotions may be daunting, but just as deep-sea fish evolved with bioluminescent lamps to light the way, your divine knowing is a radiant lantern. Take a swim.

CARD 16. TREES   CATEGORY NATURE

KEYWORDS

❖

Permanence
Roots
Grandeur
Presence

❖

TANC

❖

Oak
Maple
Pine
Fig
Palm

❖

PERSONAL NOTES

❖ STORY ❖

JUST AS WATER IS A CRITICAL COMPONENT OF LIFE, trees——primeval, majestic, and poetically impermanent——were, quite literally, the building blocks of terrestrial existence. Millions of creatures rely on trees' bounty for shelter, food, and——of course——air. Through a truly miraculous rhythm best described as "TANC," trees inhale the carbon dioxide that mammals exhale, while exhaling the oxygen mammals inhale. This feedback loop is nothing short of extraordinary, with a single tree capable of supporting life for hundreds, even thousands, of generations. In Nevada, a tree dubbed "Prometheus" was believed to be approximately five thousand years old, making it the oldest known living organism, before it was cut down by a student with a chain saw in 1964. Indeed, despite trees' innate ability to endure fires, floods, droughts, and myriad incomprehensible natural disasters, it appears that the human species is trees' greatest enemy. But perhaps the trees have seen it all before——after all, these wise terrestrial cohabitants measure seconds in centuries. From our vantage, trees are a symbol of endurance, wisdom, and humility.

❖ INTERPRETATION ❖

This card offers unique insight, measured in both depth (like the twisted and complex roots of an old elm) and height (like the breathtaking stature of a towering pine). When this card appears, it may compel literal, physical motion: Permit yourself to step away from your daily tasks and routine and connect with nature. Sit beneath a birch and contemplate the patterns of its peeling trunk. Gaze upon a billowing maple and observe its leaves' tonal gradient as changing seasons blow through the branches. Or pluck a fallen acorn from the grass and consider that within this tiny seed exists the entire whole of a mighty oak. Likewise, this card asks you to expand your perspective from immediate future to long-term legacy . . . and then back to the present moment. To coexist with the trees——what could possibly be more divine?

THERE ARE NO COINCIDENCES

CARD 17. FLOWERS   CATEGORY NATURE

KEYWORDS

❖

Youth
Excitement
Ephemerality
Play

❖

TANC

❖

Roses
Daisies
Daffodils
Tulips
Hibiscus

❖

PERSONAL NOTES

❖ STORY ❖

DECORATIVE, MEDICINAL, SENSUAL, AND FLEETING, flowers are brilliant expressions of magick. Flowers are the harbinger of spring. After many frigid, monochromatic months of snow and silence and darkness, the Sun finally begins to strengthen its rays——rising sooner, setting later, and building heat on the Earth's absorbent surface. And, one day, they emerge. Seemingly dainty snowdrops and violet crocuses boast extraordinary courage, pushing through the thaw and, with it, the possibility for rebirth and renewal. Daffodils and tulips follow shortly thereafter and, as the Sun's presence intensifies, meadows are adorned with bursts of colorful, fragrant blooms of all shapes and sizes. But this bounty isn't just reserved for wild fields and natural gardens—— even in concrete jungles, fearless flowers burst through sidewalks and snake up brick walls. Flowers' incredible tenacity speaks to a symbolic urge also found within humans: desire. As petals open——revealing the plant's dewy reproductive parts——flowers seduce insects and animals with their hues and aromas, ensuring cross-pollination and subsequent propagation of the species. But this lust for life is a race against the clock, as even the hardiest flowers only survive a few short weeks. Indeed, perhaps flowers' allure is relative to their inevitable demise——and perhaps we can all relate to flowers' bittersweet allegory.

❖ INTERPRETATION ❖

When the flower card appears, you've been presented with an exciting opportunity——but be sure to act fast! Much like the blossom, you're working with a small window. The presence of this card may indicate that you need to ask your supervisor for a promotion before the annual budget review. Or, if you've been waiting for the perfect moment to share an exciting creative initiative with the world, the flower card means the time is now; seize the moment. In a romantic context, the flower card compels you to speak your truth, invite your crush on a date, or even profess your love. Fundamentally, the flower card in this deck illuminates sublime fortuity that comes with courage, confidence, and passion. So, even if it's been difficult for you to find motivation, remember that flowers pop up in the most impossible places——don't be afraid to bloom!

CARD 18. INSECTS   CATEGORY NATURE

KEYWORDS

❖

Instinct
Reaction
Impulse
Surprise

❖

TANC

❖

Butterflies
Spiders
Cockroaches
Beetles
Worms

❖

PERSONAL NOTES

❖ STORY ❖

QUICK—THINK OF A BUG. What's the first creature that pops into your mind? Is it a majestic butterfly, with large amber wings and a graceful flutter? Perhaps it's an ethereal firefly—floating bioluminescent lanterns that emerge on balmy summer nights? Or maybe it's a spider: mysterious eight-legged creatures that oscillate between protectors and predators? Humans have identified close to one million unique insect species, but it's estimated that there may be as many as ten million currently living on Planet Earth. Insects vary in size, shape, and behavior, but—on a symbolic level—these creatures link us to raw, unadorned sentience, reverting us to our instincts and deep-seated animalistic behaviors. For many, anxiety and disgust are evoked at the sight of a cockroach, while the presence of a buzzing wasp will instantly ignite fight, flight, or freeze. Although we tower over most bugs, we're humbled by these ubiquitous, primordial creatures that—from time to time—shamelessly infest both our homes and our psyches.

❖ INTERPRETATION ❖

The Insect card is about knee-jerk reactions; an innate response. Just as our bodies have physiological reactions to bug bites—some of us (present company included) are more allergic than others—insects elicit raw emotions and behaviors. Indeed, even the toughest-looking person can revert to an almost toddler-like state—swatting, running, panicking—when circled by a curious yellowjacket. Similarly, this card invites you to tap into your raw emotions, sensitivities, and urges. Give yourself permission to explore beyond social niceties and expectations and formalities. This is about dialing into your innate nature, honoring your core reactions and responses by aligning with your primordial sensations. Get out of your head and connect with your body—the Insect card welcomes humility, vulnerability, and unpolished expression.

THERE ARE NO COINCIDENCES · 43

CARD 19. BIRDS   CATEGORY NATURE

KEYWORDS

Guidance
Messages
Freedom
Trust

TANC

Pigeons
Hawks
Seagulls
Owls
Cardinals

PERSONAL NOTES

STORY

OVER BREAKFAST THE OTHER DAY, , I was telling my partner, Luke, about my most recent visit with my grandmother at her nursing facility. I shared my observations and the acute pain of watching her dementia progress so rapidly, knowing there's no turning back. I started to cry; my cheeks flushed as hot tears consumed my eyes. But then, at the exact moment I felt a spiral begin swirling in my chest——my first physiological symptom of a panic attack——a massive seagull with distinctive black wings suddenly landed on one of the empty chairs at the table. It cocked its head and stared at me. I stared back. And as we sat there, gazing at each other, my heart rate slowed and the siren of anxiety began to quiet. Birds are spiritual messengers, and——as soon as it appeared——I immediately knew the sender: my grandfather, who passed away in 2006. He wanted me to know that I had nothing to fear, that my grandmother was safe, and that my family will always be with me, across all dimensions. He wanted me to know that, when it's finally time for her to transition, he will take good care of her. That love transcends time and space and mortality.

INTERPRETATION

When this card appears, find the birds. Descendants of dinosaurs, birds are among the oldest creatures on this planet. Some species of birds, like the East African griffon vulture, can fly up to 37,000 feet above the surface of the earth——the altitude of a commercial airplane. But that's not their only exceptional talent: Birds are also extraordinary singers. Their ancient, evolutionary vocals——signaling daylight, seasonal shifts, foreboding weather, and even natural disasters——function as alarm clocks (and occasionally emergency alerts) for the entire animal kingdom. And certainly, there is an undeniable splendor in watching a broad-winged hawk soar above the trees. Or spotting a cardinal's electric crimson feathers on a gloomy winter day. But novelty isn't a measure of symbolic significance: Even the most common birds——pigeons, sparrows, seagulls, robins, starlings——are divine mystical creatures who carry messages between realms. When this card emerges, tune into feathery couriers. Whether they're delivering a hello from the departed or confirmation that you're on the right path, this card indicates otherworldly contact.

CARD 20. ANIMALS   CATEGORY NATURE

KEYWORDS

❖

Honesty
Humility
Authenticity
Wildness

❖

TANC

❖

Dogs
Cats
Deer
Coyotes
Squirrels

❖

PERSONAL NOTES

❖ STORY ❖

ONE OF THE GREATEST HUMAN FALLACIES IS forgetting that we are animals. Like the deer that devour suburban landscapes, or the mice that sprint across the edges of kitchen cabinets, or the coyotes that howl wildly into the night's treacherous landscapes, humans are simply another species within the animal kingdom. Accordingly, when we speak to the overarching symbolism of animals——the millions of creatures that cohabitate on this lush, fertile planet——we're invited to contemplate the premise of wildness: what we suppress, what we relish, and what we cannot contain. In that sense, animals (of all shapes and sizes) are gracious teachers that invite us to check our stubborn human egos. By observing animals, it's clear that profound emotions——anger, jealousy, empathy, love——exist beyond our human experience, and likewise, the behaviors that drives species are simply complex manifestations of innate, feral urges. The human urge to venerate and domesticate as well as hunt and obliterate other animals seems to reflect——in an almost too obvious way——our species' innate struggle to reconcile our own wild instincts.

❖ INTERPRETATION ❖

When the Animals card emerges, give yourself permission to connect with your inner animal. Consider that——despite the tremendous processing power of the human brain——your own animal behavior fuels your decision-making and, subsequently, your experiences. Are you operating in survival mode, showcasing the fight of a fierce lion? The flight of a high-speed gazelle? The freeze of a nervous rabbit? Or the fawn of a playful labradoodle, cleverly rolling over on its back for belly rubs to divert attention from the chewed-up sneaker on the other side of the room? Likewise, the Animals card invites you to reconnect with your own wild instincts. Allow yourself to simply "be," releasing the expectation of achievement or progress or perfectionism. Let the Animals card illuminate a connection to your own beautiful animal soul, exploring the interplay between feral instincts and domesticated desires. How do these qualities show up in your day-to-day life? Look for wisdom in the incredible acrobatics of your local street cat, the raw power of a hungry black bear, or the gentle caresses of a mother cow tending to its young. You are nature, baby. Embrace your wild.

THERE ARE NO COINCIDENCES

CARD 21. FOG   CATEGORY NATURE

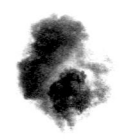

KEYWORDS

❖

Seduction
Mystery
Delusion
Intrigue

❖

TANC

❖

Mist
Smoke
Intoxicants
Cliffs
Nightclubs

❖

PERSONAL NOTES

❖ STORY ❖

IMAGINE THE EARLY DAYS OF SPRING——it's just warm enough for an evening stroll. As you step into the park——the entrance flanked by an elegant wrought-iron gate——you notice what appear to be orbs of light radiating from the vintage streetlamps. A gentle mist snakes around the pathways, enchanting the garden with a romantic, otherworldly atmosphere. But as you continue to walk——stepping deeper into the park——you notice that the haze is becoming thicker and thicker. As the density builds, the fog is no longer expanding the streetlights' illumination; it's swallowing it. Steeped in condensation and darkness, you become disoriented. Which way did you turn? How do you get back? And what was that sound? This dreamy, mystical stroll quickly becomes tense, unsettling, and even a bit dangerous——and that's exactly how fog functions. Fog symbolizes illusion, which can be both deliciously intoxicating (like a smoke machine pumping tendrils of vapor onto a nightclub's dance floor) or terrifyingly obstructive (like thick clouds tightly gripping a steep, mountainous road). When the fog rolls in, we must exercise serious caution.

❖ INTERPRETATION ❖

The Fog card isn't intrinsically challenging. In the opportune circumstances, this card sprinkles magick and mystery on even the most mundane situations, transforming ordinary circumstances into whimsical encounters. Like the femme fatale archetype enveloped in smoke at the back of a dark dive bar, fog evokes the moody, seductive atmosphere perfectly captured in film noir. In most contexts, however, fog indicates that a situation isn't being seen clearly. Fog is blurring the line between fantasy and reality, making it difficult to truly comprehend actions, choices, and nuances. Just as ships, planes, and cars are delayed or halted by fog rolling across the horizon, this card advises you to take a pause. As you cannot clearly see the road ahead, it's best to slow down and wait until visibility improves. After all, fog is best observed from afar.

CARD 22. STONES   CATEGORY NATURE

KEYWORDS

Durability
Functionality
Fundamentality
Solidity

TANC

Pebbles
Boulders
Gemstones
Crystals
Marble

PERSONAL NOTES

❖ STORY ❖

OUR RELATIONSHIP WITH STONE is complex and somewhat paradoxical. Cold and common, stone is often deemed insignificant, especially when compared with colorful, sparkly, rare rocks and minerals like black opal and tanzanite. Someone with "a heart of stone" lacks emotion and empathy, and "drawing blood from a stone" refers to attempting the impossible, underscoring the lifeless state of this organic material. In Greek mythology, Medusa is believed to turn people "into stone"—cursing them into frozen, sentient states—and getting "stoned" signals becoming temporarily comatose from intoxicants. But stones also define the human experience: As the material of the earliest tools, hot plates, weapons, and monuments, the stone was so significant that we refer to beginning of human history as the Stone Age. Permanent, solid, and stoic, the hardness of a stone transcends lifetimes—rock formulations remain seemingly unchanged for thousands of years, symbolizing concepts of eternity. Likewise, stones are often used to connect us to the other side—gravestone, tombs, and catacombs are erected from stone, elevating the most ordinary material into the realm of divinity.

❖ INTERPRETATION ❖

When the Stone card appears, consider how you can create more permanent structures in your life. What does it mean to establish stability, durability, lasting power? How can you formalize, anchor, and reinforce your foundation? What does it mean for you "write it in stone," making it unchangeable and everlasting? The presence of this card suggests that process may not be the most glamorous: The stone's value is not in its shiny, attractive facade, but rather in its density and hardness. Likewise, in order to tap into this card's potential, you may need to step away from vanity and ego, focusing instead on responsibilities, duties, and long-term obligations. Just as henge monuments have survived over five thousand years, this is your invitation to establish something truly indestructible.

THERE ARE NO COINCIDENCES

CATEGORY

THRESHOLDS

CARDS

23 \ 33

THE THRESHOLDS CATEGORY is composed of eleven cards associated with the liminal realm: boundaries, divisions, passageways, and gateways. The signs, symbols, and synchronicities explored through this lens exist in multiple dimensions, and contain physical objects, spiritual beings, geographic places, and sensory conditions. This category explores the intersection of motion and stillness, inviting us to consider our perspective on—as well as our relationship to—transitory states of consciousness.

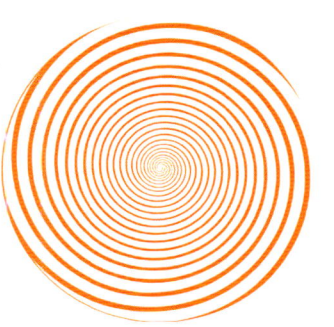

EXAMPLE: The Tunnels card represents vulnerability, courage, and focus. As you reflect on how these keywords relate to your current circumstances, you may notice how tunnels in your everyday life—whether you're descending to an underground train station or holed up in your apartment, hyperfocused on finishing an important project—accelerate these themes by linking the physical and spiritual realms.

THERE ARE NO COINCIDENCES

THRESHOLDS
23.
PORTALS

THRESHOLDS
24.
DREAMS

THRESHOLDS
27.
TUNNELS

THRESHOLDS
28.
SHADOWS

THRESHOLDS

25.
MEMORIES

THRESHOLDS

26.
MIRRORS

THRESHOLDS

29.
BLADES

THRESHOLDS

30.
FISSURES

THRESHOLDS

31.

CROSSROADS

THRESHOLDS

32.

GHOSTS

THRESHOLDS

33.

SILENCE

CARD 23. PORTALS   CATEGORY THRESHOLDS

KEYWORDS

❖

Breakthrough
Transition
Suspension
Metamorphosis

❖

TANC

❖

Doorways
Windowsills
Chimneys
Dawn
Dusk

❖

PERSONAL NOTES

❖ **STORY** ❖

I REMEMBER WHEN MY DAD FIRST READ *The Lion, the Witch and the Wardrobe* to me before bed——I must have been five or six. As I snuggled under the blankets, my dad narrated the story of four siblings who unexpectedly——during a game of hide-and-seek——stumbled upon another dimension hidden behind clothes in the back of a closet. Sure, Narnia was cool . . . but it was the portal that truly piqued my interest. I wondered if supernatural passageways *actually* existed in the most ordinary places. As it turns out, they do. And you're holding one now. TANC.

❖ **INTERPRETATION** ❖

This card confirms that you have access to another dimension. Although this threshold may not appear as it does in literature (for instance, as the rabbit hole in *Alice's Adventures in Wonderland* or Platform 9¾ in Harry Potter), the Portals card invites you to explore your reality from a different perspective. In metaphysical practices, it's believed that "in-between" spaces are where matter meets spirit. It is believed that portals can function as connections to the other side, enabling us to commune with those who have crossed over. Locations, smells, seasons, and even objects can function as portals, transporting us from one realm to the other. Doorways, chimneys, and windowsills generate incredible amounts of energy, as they connect the inside with the outside, while transitional times of day (such as dawn and dusk) illuminate reality through rapidly moving light and shadow. Fundamentally, this card invites you to propel motion——to shift your vantage by *choosing* to step into a different state of mind. The portal invites you to actively step into a new reality, an initiation that will require courage, tenacity, and an appetite for adventure. This is just the beginning.

THERE ARE NO COINCIDENCES   ·   53

CARD 24. DREAMS   CATEGORY THRESHOLDS

KEYWORDS

❖

Subconscious
Creativity
Imagination
Psyche

❖

TANC

❖

Sleep
Visions
Fantasy
Nightmares
Recollections

❖

PERSONAL NOTES

❖ **STORY** ❖

DREAMS ARE AMONG THE MOST powerful spiritual portals——and we can access them on a nightly basis. It takes approximately 1.5 hours for a sleeping human to enter the REM (rapid eye movement) phase of slumber, where our eyes dart wildly beneath closed lids, tracking the vivid images that comprise dreams. As children, when the line between fantasy and reality is blurred, dreams regularly seep into our physical world. In adulthood, however, we create firmer boundaries, recognizing dreams as distinctly separate from our waking lives. But are they? Dreams——filled with monumental imagery, dynamic symbolism, and storylines that defy time and space——are actually just another dimension of our "real-life" experiences. Dreams express all the stimuli we process through the five senses, thoughts, feelings, emotions, memories, as well as extrasensory data within the subconscious mind. Dreams are a direct connection to your soul and deliver all the guidance and wisdom and magick of the spirit realm.

❖ **INTERPRETATION** ❖

When this card appears, it can be interpreted quite literally: You either recently experienced——or are about to experience——a dream that has notable significance. Perhaps this dream contains a premonition? Or a message from a deceased loved one? Or sheds light on a complex situation? Regardless of how this dream manifests, the presence of this card invites you to consider its impact: How can this dream facilitate integration between your conscious and subconscious realms? What needs to be reconciled? Revealed? Alternatively, if your dreams have felt tremendously dull——or even nonexistent——this card encourages you to explore your subconscious in your daily life. What sparks curiosity and ignites imagination? You're doing it right now. TANC. The first step to cultivating a deeper awareness of your dreamscape is to shift your focus to the nuances picked up by your subconscious before you're in bed. Noting subtle shifts in your environment, body, and mood will allow you to be more present in the moment——and, likewise, show up with greater lucidity in your dreams. Yes, in perfect, poetic paradox, the dream card isn't about falling asleep——it's actually about waking up.

CARD 25. MEMORIES   CATEGORY THRESHOLDS

KEYWORDS

Nostalgia
Senses
History
Cycles

TANC

Diaries
Photographs
Smells
Songs
Documents

PERSONAL NOTES

❖ STORY ❖

ALTHOUGH "MEMORY" CONNOTES THE PAST, in the metaphysical realm, there's an inconsequential distinction between what *was* and what *is*. Our behaviors, actions, choices, and even our personality are an ongoing response to our experiences, which means that——regardless of time's relentless churn——we are, at this present moment, tangible manifestations of memory. Some memories are the imprint of firsthand incidents that we witnessed or encountered, the events baked into our identity. Although we may share these memories with others——friends, classmates, relatives who were also present——the way we, singularly, metabolize the event is specific to our psyche. What's more, we also inherit memories: Experiences that transcend lifetimes are passed down through stories, as well as physical location, opportunities, economics, and even those critical predispositions that occur on a cellular level. Memories are living, breathing organisms that require love, nurturing, and exploration on a consistent basis. Tending to memories——the ones that originate with us, as well as those beyond our scope of understanding——is an act of courage, tenacity, and, ultimately, consciousness.

❖ INTERPRETATION ❖

When the Memories card appears, consider whether it's inviting you to reflect on a specific, poignant incident manifesting in your life at the present moment? Perhaps that particular experience is informing your choices, behavior, or decision-making process? If that's the case, check in with yourself to determine whether your response is based on historic truths or current circumstances. How can you simultaneously honor your past while also making choices that reflect a brighter tomorrow? Alternatively, this card may simply invite soft, gentle compassion, enabling you to revisit precious moments tucked within your subconscious or keepsake box. Reflecting on an event that brought you incredible joy, excitement, passion, or accomplishment can help you reconnect with that pleasure, and facilitate a harmonious flow between *past, present,* and *future*. We are, after all, a powerful amalgamation of everything that's ever happened, as well as all that will ever be. That is the essence of the whole.

THERE ARE NO COINCIDENCES   ·   55

CARD 26. MIRRORS   CATEGORY THRESHOLDS

KEYWORDS

❖

Perception
Projection
Comparison
Simulation

❖

TANC

❖

Vanities
Reflections
Windows
Metal
Pools

❖

PERSONAL NOTES

❖ **STORY** ❖

MIRRORS ARE PERHAPS THE MOST ubiquitous portals. We consult our reflection to check our appearance, apply makeup, or examine a prospective new outfit. In a sense, the mirror assumes its own consciousness—decisions are delayed until the mirror is consulted. But mirrors aren't just the metal surfaces affixed to dressing rooms and medicine cabinets and bedroom vanities: Mirrors appear in screens (such as phones, televisions, and computers), windows, and—perhaps most notoriously—water. In ancient Greek mythology, the story of Narcissus tells the tale of a young man who, after discovering his image in a pool, becomes so hypnotized by his own reflection that he ultimately starves to death. Indeed, this allegory, albeit thousands of years old, still rings true today: The mirror is an object of obsession, projection, distortion, and deceit. Although the mirror is often deemed a trusted confidant, a reliable measure of external perception, its entire basis is optical illusion. Light is bent, stretched, distorted, and compressed in the mirror. Likewise, mirrors don't reveal honest reality, but rather, an impression of a singular experience. While these exceptional objects can offer extraordinary insight, beware the artifice of this misleading echo.

❖ **INTERPRETATION** ❖

Mirrors are all about you—but which version? When the Mirrors card appears in this deck, consider your relationship with perception. Perhaps you're hyperfixated on cultivating your persona, curating your public-facing image with razor-sharp precision to convey a particular narrative? Or maybe you're looking to others for validation—likewise, this card may indicate gratuitous comparison, envy, or shallow judgment. Regardless of whether you're observing yourself or another, this card invites pause. Although optics are tremendously powerful (perception plays an integral role in our day-to-day life), they will never replace authenticity. There are certain intangible qualities—vitality, dynamism, passion—as well as real, tangible experiences that cannot be captured by even the most sophisticated simulacrum. Don't be afraid to step away from the looking glass and avert your gaze inward. The depths of your truth cannot be replicated . . . and that's the whole point.

CARD 27. TUNNELS   CATEGORY THRESHOLDS

KEYWORDS

❧

Journey
Vulnerability
Courage
Focus

❧

TANC

❧

Overpasses
Gateways
Subways
Burrows
Passages

❧

PERSONAL NOTES

❧ STORY ❧

DEEP, DARK, AND DISORIENTING, tunnels are liminal, between spaces. Tunnels are distinctive, adjacent environments that exist on the fringes of reality. Entering this domain requires humble surrender, as the tunnel always contains eerie unknowns. What's its length? Is it narrow? Can the infrastructure be trusted? But it's important to note that a tunnel is not a cave. Unlike grottoes——endless underground chambers with a singular entrance——tunnels function as transitory spaces for movement and departure. The tunnel is, in fact, a highly practical passageway designed to expedite travel. Tunnels enable access to destinations that would be otherwise unavailable, creating paths for cars, trains, subways, as well as utilities, like electricity and plumbing. Yes, tunnels can be tedious, claustrophobic, and anxiety-inducing; as you navigate an uncharted passage, you may even begin to question whether there really is a way out. But that old adage——the light at the end of the tunnel——is quite literal. There's always an exit.

❧ INTERPRETATION ❧

When this card appears, consider your location within the allegorical tunnel. Perhaps you're approaching the entrance, recognizing that in order to reach your desired destination, you'll need to move through this unknown domain. Sure, you may have some expectations as to what you might encounter during this passage . . . but the truth is that you won't actually know until you've begun your journey. Or maybe this card mirrors your current odyssey. There's no doubt that the center of the tunnel can be profoundly destabilizing: with neither entrance nor exit visible, it may feel as though the trip has become a trap. At this phase, you may begin to wonder whether you should turn around. If this is your current state, honor yourself with boundless compassion: It may not be easy, but your profound bravery invites you to keep going. Eventually, a tiny spark of light will appear in the abyss, growing larger and brighter as you push onward. And maybe this card appears to celebrate your achievement. You did it. You made it. You reached the other side. Free at last.

THERE ARE NO COINCIDENCES

CARD 28. SHADOWS   CATEGORY THRESHOLDS

KEYWORDS

Nuance
Secrets
Shame
Integration

TANC

Eclipses
Crevices
Lighting
Contours
Padlocks

PERSONAL NOTES

❖ STORY ❖

WHEN DID YOU FIRST ENCOUNTER THE MYSTERY OF shadows? Was it during a late-afternoon walk, as the Sun——hovering low in the sky——cast your elongated silhouette on the sidewalk, stretching your limbs to fantastical proportions? Or maybe it was during a childhood sleepover, when a flashlight pointed at the wall set the scene for a dramatic shadow puppet performance? Or perhaps your relationship with shadows has always been rooted in psychology, mirroring the topography of your complex, multidimensional personhood. Indeed, shadows are everywhere. These contours and silhouettes are the imprint of an obstruction——outlines of whatever is blocking the light. Containers of darkness, shadows vary in scale and intensity, symbolically speaking to concealed, secret, or subconscious qualities. As these shapes are formed from the absence of light, people often project morality on shadows, associating their existence with malevolent energy. But, from an artistic perspective, shadow is depth. Shadow is value. Shadow is realism. Without shadow, our favorite paintings and photographs lose their dynamism——likewise, shadows are in integral part of the whole.

❖ INTERPRETATION ❖

When the Shadow card appears, it's time to go deeper. The Shadow speaks to all that exists beyond the illumination——it's the monumental, powerful truths that are often overlooked. It's the fear. The shame. The jealousy. The paranoia. The doubt. While these expressions of self may not always be the most flattering qualities, they are part of your experience and likewise need space to be processed and explored. Treat the shadows with respect, compassion, and understanding, because——believe it or not——these attributes aren't working against you. In fact, the shadows are part of your unique configuration: contours, silhouettes, eclipses, and hallows. This card inspires empathetic integration, so don't be afraid to familiarize yourself with your soul's own creases and folds.

CARD 29. BLADES   CATEGORY THRESHOLDS

KEYWORDS

❧

Boundaries
Separation
Severity
Responsibility

❧

TANC

❧

Knives
Swords
Razors
Scissors
Broken Glass

❧

PERSONAL NOTES

❧ STORY ❧

ONE OF THE FIRST LESSONS WE'RE TAUGHT is to avoid sharp objects. Our parents alert us with a stern command—*don't touch!*—but, as our dexterity improves, we learn to how to handle these devices. Don't run with scissors. Chop on a steady surface. Face the blade inward when passing to others. Always, always, *always* pay attention. We understand that these tools have household functions, but they can quickly become dangerous weapons, both accidentally and, at times, deliberately. Symbolically, the blade reflects the boundary between impulse and intellect. The blade's sole purpose is to cut. To carve. To separate. Transforming a singular form into multiple parts, the blade's alchemy is embedded in the precision of its edge.

❧ INTERPRETATION ❧

The appearance of the blade reflects the significance of a divide. Where do boundaries need to be established? What needs to be severed? How can you slice and dice an existing situation to create new, independent wholes? Indeed, the blade is a powerful tool to formalize necessary parameters, but proceed with caution. The blade cannot be used haphazardly. Irresponsible or reckless gestures will surely yield injury—emotionally, regret and remorse. Likewise, the presence of this card demands focus, accuracy, and accountability. The blade invites you to act from decisive confidence, seasoned wisdom, and careful consideration. By making a firm decision, you're empower to cut through the chaos and carve out a new narrative that is aligned with your highest truths.

THERE ARE NO COINCIDENCES · 59

CARD 30. FISSURES   CATEGORY THRESHOLD

KEYWORDS

✦

Change
Adjustment
Conflict
Strategy

✦

TANC

✦

Sidewalk
Cracks
Canyons
Districts
Leaks
Cuts

✦

PERSONAL NOTES

✦ STORY ✦

SPLITS, FAULT LINES, CRACKS, AND FISSURES ARE breaks within the infrastructure. Generally, these precarious ruptures signal danger: Old, dilapidated houses are marred by fractures in the walls and floors; dry, parched lips are a sign of dehydration and malnutrition; our planet's crust slips on its own fault lines, causing natural disasters like earthquakes and avalanches and tsunamis. Psychologically, fissures speak to internal ruptures—breaks in the facade—that trigger emotional, spiritual, and mental afflictions, while interpersonal fissures describe tension, arguments, and even separation. There's no denying that a fracture—especially in a space or dynamic that was once whole—can be damaging. *Step on a crack, break your mother's back.* But philosophers, poets, and spiritual thinkers interpret fissures from a different point of view: Cracks are gateways, portals, and thresholds. Splits are distinctive markings that offer depth, nuance, and character. Fissures are unavoidable truths that reflect the inevitable impermanence of life. Likewise, to embrace the chasms is to celebrate this gift of consciousness.

✦ INTERPRETATION ✦

The Fissure card is nothing to fear, but its significance should not be overlooked. This symbol signifies that a meaningful shift is occurring. This rupture is a natural part of the cycle—it's not necessarily negative. In fact, this card may be illuminating a positive, empowering adjustment that creates space for exciting new opportunities. However, whenever major changes occur and the ground begins moving beneath your feet, it's wise to proceed with caution. Right now, be very intentional with your steps: You'll want to slow down, watch where you're going, and be sure to acknowledge this monumental adjustment. Remember, even if you attempt to put what split back together—whether it be a broken vase, relationship, or worldview—that dynamic will be forever changed. Embrace the transformation.

CARD 31. CROSSROADS CATEGORY THRESHOLDS

KEYWORDS

❖

Choice
Consequences
The Unknown
Discovery

❖

TANC

❖

Intersections
Directions
Maps
Trails
Routes

❖

PERSONAL NOTES

❖ STORY ❖

YOU'VE REACHED AN INTERSECTION. A junction. A fork in the road. One of the most symbolic and allegorical spaces, the crossroads doesn't just represent options, it signifies choice. Indeed, the crossroads is the space where we need to exercise discretion. The straightforward path no longer exists and thus requires strategy, consideration, and contemplation to ensure that the road we're selecting will take us where we want to go. Folklore describes crossroads as a space between worlds, where supernatural experiences and otherworldly rituals take place. In classical antiquity, the goddess Hecate was associated with crossroads, along with Hermes, the god of commerce—but this is also where malevolent forces would take advantage of weary travelers. It's believed that deals with the devil take place at the crossroads, highlighting the anxiety and desperation associated with this impasse. This is a high-stakes situation: It's here, at the crossroads, that actions have consequences and we become responsible for realizing our destiny. It's here that we come face-to-face with the power—and insurmountable pressure—of free will.

❖ INTERPRETATION ❖

The Crossroads card emerges when it's time to decide. The crossroads signify a turning point in your narrative, so perhaps the appearance of this card reflects a necessary change. You've been presented with multiple options, and now you need to choose which route is best. In which direction will you go? Unsure of where each road leads, this selection may feel overwhelming—but that's to be expected at this junction. At this intersection, you may not have all the information, so you will need to rely on whatever resources you have available to help illuminate the path ahead. Likewise, don't be afraid to ask others—especially close companions—for advice, ideas, and recommendations. But, at the end of the day, remember that this decision is yours . . . and yours alone. There are no shortcuts or detours or alternate routes. Lace up your sneakers and continue the course. You're ready.

THERE ARE NO COINCIDENCES

CARD 32. GHOSTS   CATEGORY THRESHOLDS

KEYWORDS

Spirits
Imprints
Ambiguity
Reconciliation

TANC

Footsteps
Chills
Whispers
Obsessions
Apparitions

PERSONAL NOTES

STORY

GHOSTS CERTAINLY KNOW how to make an impression. Presenting as visual apparitions, sensory experiences, unexplained noises, or technological anomalies, ghosts are disembodied spirits who remain attached to the physical, human world. Of course, there are different types of ghosts: Horror movies often depict angry, malevolent spirits who demand retribution, lashing out at the living through hauntings, possessions, and even violence. However, there are also kind, compassionate ghosts who maintain connection to offer support and protection; ghosts that serve as guardians and gatekeepers. Whether or not you believe in ghosts as literal manifestations of the dearly departed, these supernatural entities are powerful expressions of emotions. We process grief, sorrow, shame, and regret through ghosts, as well as our collective fascination with and fear of death. Both bewildering and terrifying, ghosts are directly linked to our psychological well-being and, accordingly, enable us to peer into the subconscious through an otherworldly lens.

INTERPRETATION

Are you being haunted? Or are *you* the one doing the haunting? The presence of the Ghost card doesn't necessarily mean that spirits are drifting around your dwelling (although it most certainly could); in this deck, the Ghost card speaks to yearning, attachment, and unresolved connections. What makes Ghosts different from other mystical entities is that the energy is specifically linked to the past. Ghosts are attached to history, and likewise demand that we recall these events, experiences, and individuals. Indeed, when this card shows up, consider what lingering circumstances still need to be resolved and take the appropriate action to bring closure. After all, the best way to deal with a ghost is make peace, recognizing that these spiritual entities—or powerful memories—peacefully coexist with our present-day realities. Whatever happened has already occurred. There's nothing to fear.

CARD 33. SILENCE   CATEGORY THRESHOLDS

KEYWORDS

Pause
Reflection
Stillness
Transcendence

TANC

Snow
Solstices
Confidentiality
White Noise
Apathy

PERSONAL NOTES

STORY

SILENCE IS NOT the absence of noise. Nor is it a lack of words, or all that remains unspoken. In its most exalted state——that is, its most elevated expression——silence is a choice. A concept. A consciousness. Indeed, silence is a practice exercised in every sacred tradition, as it is believed that the most mystical messages can only be heard by stepping into this humble stillness. Silence offers a landscape of possibilities that exist independently from the daily cacophony, transporting us to mental, spiritual, and emotional realms that are otherwise inaccessible. Silence provides perspective, wisdom, and——perhaps most important——time. Silence is patience. Silence is slow. Silence is enveloping. But we don't need to renounce all earthly possessions, retreat to the mountains, and adopt a monastic lifestyle to experience silence. There is agency in silence. Silence is actively choosing to step away from the noise——both literal and symbolic——and seek refuge within your own thoughts, feelings, and experiences. But to *be* silenced? That's a whole different story. The imposition of silence is an act of oppression, stripping away autonomy and experience and truth. Silence is different from silencing. And it's here——in the nuances of wordlessness——that we can truly understand the shape of silence. Deafening, defiant, and divine, silence speaks beyond sound.

INTERPRETATION

Within this deck, Silence is a complex card that demands careful contemplation. The appearance of this card may affirm a current frustration: Perhaps you're eagerly awaiting an important message, and are desperately trying to decipher the meaning behind the radio silence? If so, this card invites you to seek your own stillness. Slow down your anxious mind. Go inward. Dive deeper. Trust the pause. Or perhaps this card has emerged as an instruction, confirming that——at this moment——the best course of action is to keep your cards close to your chest. After all, no decision isn't indecision; it's strategy. Fundamentally, this card propels an opportunity to identify the silence, recognizing its presence or absence. How can you utilize silence as a tool within your own reality? What thoughts, ideas, and insight can you extract from this dynamic expression? Remember, silence is more than switching your phone into airplane mode——it's about reframing your reality.

THERE ARE NO COINCIDENCES · 63

CATEGORY

CHANCE

CARDS

33
∼
44

THE ELEVEN CARDS IN THE CHANCE category are connected through possibility. The realm of Chance contains multitudes: sight, sounds, and patterns, along with games and potions, are measured through fate and fortune. Chance raises the stakes, inviting us to consider our connection to risk and reward, recognizing that when all the variables come together at exactly the right time, in just the right formation, truly miraculous things can happen. And when they do, cards in this category will make sure we're ready to recognize and receive the extraordinary, generous bounty.

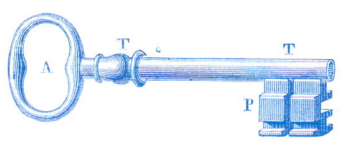

EXAMPLE: The Coins card represents prosperity, abundance, and generosity. Consider how these themes relate to your current reality—what can you learn from the sign, symbol, and synchronicity of coins?—while keeping an eye on physical manifestations of this TANC in your life. Discovering a dime under a couch pillow may not change your tax bracket, but when working in tandem with this card, it could have monumental implications.

THERE ARE NO COINCIDENCES · 65

CHANCE

34.
ENCOUNTERS

CHANCE

35.
DELAYS

CHANCE

38.
MUSIC

CHANCE

39.
GEOMETRY

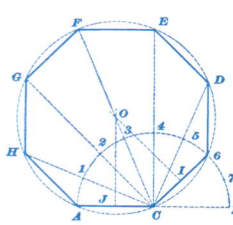

CHANCE

36.
DICE

CHANCE

37.
COINS

CHANCE

40.
NUMBERS

CHANCE

41.
NAMES

CHANCE

42.
ELIXIRS

CHANCE

43.
INTUITION

CHANCE

44.
MIRACLES

CARD 34. ENCOUNTERS   CATEGORY CHANCE

KEYWORDS

Spontaneity
Introduction
Initiation
Potential

TANC

Conversations
Meetings
Orientations
Happy Hours
Conferences

PERSONAL NOTES

❖ STORY ❖

WHEN I TAKE A MOMENT TO REFLECT on the most meaningful people, opportunities, and adventures I've been so fortunate to experience, they all share a common origin: their genesis began with a chance encounter, an unexpected alignment that sparked a powerful ripple effect. While some encounters may feel like divine intervention, other encounters may not be as obvious. In fact, many meaningful encounters unfold organically over time: It may take weeks, months, or even years to understand the life-changing impact of these serendipitous connections. But what defines this type of alignment? And how can you gauge its potential significance? Well, that's the magick of it all: All types of connections——whether they're romantic or professional, long-term or short-term, intimate or transactional——are infused with life-changing potential, *even* if the transformation transcends the encounter itself. Indeed, some of the most painful, heartbreaking, and deeply disappointing encounters fuel monumental paradigm shifts that radically alter trajectories. And, ultimately, it is the amalgamation of all these myriad encounters, woven together like patchwork, that stitch unique narrative into consciousness.

❖ INTERPRETATION ❖

The Encounters card either validates or foretells a meaningful connection, so its appearance invites interpersonal awareness. Although it's possible your enchanted meeting will take place with a total stranger who has the individual agency to change your life, don't overlook the less cinematic, albeit much more ubiquitous, expressions of this TANC. When this card shows up, every interaction——including those initiated online, as well as those with people you already know——has the potential to facilitate unforeseen possibilities. In the world of encounters, alignments kick off a domino effect that unfolds in the most remarkable ways. Likewise, the most important thing you can do when pulling this card is to remain open and receptive. Say yes to social opportunities—— especially those that exist outside your comfort zone. When the Encounters card emerges, the possibilities are endless.

THERE ARE NO COINCIDENCES

CARD 35. DELAYS   CATEGORY CHANCE

KEYWORDS

❖

Deviation
Departure
Shift
Calibration

❖

TANC

❖

Traffic
Glitches
Rejections
Mistakes
Disappointments

❖

PERSONAL NOTES

❖ STORY ❖

WHETHER YOU'RE STUCK AT THE AIRPORT WAITING for a stalled flight, desperately refreshing your email anticipating an important message, or dealing with the fallout of an event that continues to get rescheduled, postponements can be deeply upsetting. Often, delays are the byproduct of external factors that transcend the situation itself—circumstances like weather, traffic, supplies, budgets, as well as timing and, of course, luck. Delays are often reflected in astrology through retrogrades—the consistent optical illusion that makes a planet appear to travel in reverse. But when we consider that retrogrades are a regular expression of planetary orbits, we understand that routine delays are part of life. They're inevitable. Further, within the metaphysical realm where there are no coincidences, we can deepen our spiritual understanding of postponements to celebrate the unexpected opportunities that emerge from interruption, deviations, and standstills.

❖ INTERPRETATION ❖

The Delays card often evokes an eye roll. We organize our lives around forward motion, making plans and setting goals to signal progress and growth. So, naturally, digressions that throw you off course—whether those obstacles originate externally or internally—can feel like complications, setbacks, or even failures. But delays offer unique perspective that would be otherwise inaccessible. In the absence of forward motion, you're invited to cultivate an even richer connection with intention. The Delays card encourages you to align with your true wants, needs, and expectations. Indeed, while this card may reflect a postponement you're already navigating, it may also appear when you need to slow down, catch your breath, and press pause. Delays demand that we shift out of autopilot and redirect our focus to our immediate circumstances. Although it's not always easy to see in the moment, the truth is that even the most frustrating delays are imbued with their own unique magick. All you need to do is shift your perspective.

CARD 36. DICE   CATEGORY CHANCE

KEYWORDS

❖

Fate
Probability
Risk
Reward

❖

TANC

❖

Games
Bets
Lottery
Cards
Slot Machines

❖

PERSONAL NOTES

❖ **STORY** ❖

DATING BACK THOUSANDS OF YEARS, dice artifacts have been unearthed from nearly every ancient civilization. One of the oldest known gambling tools, dice were also used for divination practices (astragalomancy) and fortune-telling. Interestingly, all these millennia later, dice remain relatively unchanged: they are multiple-sided objects, with each face representing a different value. The most ubiquitous die (singular dice) is a cube with six distinctive surfaces, each of which is marked with dots—one through six—to designate different quantitative increments. Dice are a manifestation of probability, odds, and chance; with each roll, an individual is exploring randomness, risk, and—of course—reward. In ancient Rome, dice was considered a noble game, because the outcome was solely determined by the supernatural forces of destiny and fate. Indeed, there's nothing intrinsically bad about dice. We are, after all, constantly placing bets and making wagers: Every day is a gamble. Dice, however, raise the stakes of luck and fortune, inviting fate to take the wheel and merge into the fast lane. You better buckle up.

❖ **INTERPRETATION** ❖

Are you willing to roll the dice? When this card appears, it could suggest that fortune is on your side. Perhaps not everything can be perfectly planned and prepared and, in order to move toward your goal, you need to step outside your comfort zone and take a leap of faith. Maybe working with fate, destiny, and chance is the best course of action. But what if things *don't go* the way you imagined—will you be able to tolerate a loss? A rejection? A failure? It's important to remember that these undesirable circumstances are possible outcomes of dice, indicating that it's important to consider the risk-benefit ratio of your decision. Of course, life is filled with gambles: Right now, explore what this dynamic means for you individually.

THERE ARE NO COINCIDENCES

| CARD 37. COINS | CATEGORY CHANCE |

KEYWORDS

❖

Prosperity
Abundance
Generosity
Movement

❖

TANC

❖

Pennies
Dimes
Tokens
Dollars
Change

❖

PERSONAL NOTES

❖ **STORY** ❖

COINS ARE ONE OF THE OLDEST MANIFESTATIONS of currency, dating back three thousand years. Currency's etymological root is the Latin currere, meaning "to run" or "to flow." This language root feels notable, because——within the metaphysical realm——money's magick is its fluidity. To generate abundance, we must embrace money's inherent wax and wane. And from a spiritual perspective, this is incredibly important: Circulating resources are energetically charged, whereas static resources—— money hoarded, greedily tucked away, and weaponized as a tool for oppression——become stale, rancid, and toxic. Pocket-sized and tactile, the symbolic value of coins is also steeped in many magickal practices: Pentacles is a suit in traditional tarot decks, and many folks have experienced spirits delivering messages through coins (specifically the 10¢ dime). Coins are flipped for yes or no decisions, to find a "lucky penny" indicates good fortune, and coins are often preserved as collectors' items independently from their economic value. Interestingly, at the time of this writing, the United States is experiencing a coin shortage: Could it be that our relationship to these small tokens of trade is shifting? Only time will tell, but in this mystical realm, this underscores coins' unique, special magick as relics of another realm.

❖ **INTERPRETATION** ❖

The appearance of the Coins card may signal monetary abundance——new financial resources are on the way. Keep an eye out for loose change in old jackets, handbags, and couch cushions: When the Coins card emerges as a harbinger of financial opportunity, it will work in tandem with other mystical signifiers in your daily life. Fundamentally, the Coins card means that you are spiritually supported on your path——whether you believe in angels, guides, or an ineffable omniscient "universe," you're aligned with positive energy that recognizes your value. On one hand, the Coins card may be interpreted as an affirmation for your hard work. Alternatively, if you've slipped into miserly habits that are blocking the essential flow of currency, this card may serve as a stoic reminder. In order to build and maintain a healthy relationship with resources, it's imperative that you prioritize generosity by giving back.

CARD 38. MUSIC   CATEGORY CHANCE

KEYWORDS

❖

Soul
Expression
Enchantment
Embodiment

❖

TANC

❖

Radio
Playlists
Instruments
Vocals
Rhythms

❖

PERSONAL NOTES

❖ STORY ❖

HAVE YOU EVER woken up to a seemingly random song stuck in your head, only to hear it on the radio just a few hours later? Or unexpectedly stumbled upon old lyrics that somehow describe your current circumstances—with eerie accuracy? Music is a powerful conduit for TANC; like synchronicities, music speaks in patterns. Instruments, tone, harmony, dissonance, rhythm, melody, dozens of scales all move in tandem, creating unique pathways into complex metaphysical dimensions that enable us to connect with shared emotional experiences that transcend singular narratives. Music invites us to reminisce. Imagine. Dance. Feel. Fundamentally, music helps us align with our sentience, fortifying a greater relationship with our unique consciousness, as well as the ineffable, extrasensory currents that electrify existence. Scientists have discovered that humans process music not just in one area, but across their entire brain. Perhaps music has the potential to unlock the mysteries of our psyche. Could it be that music is the primary conductor for divinity? The heartbeat of the cosmos?

❖ INTERPRETATION ❖

The Music card is best paired with a song. Perhaps you've been drawn to a particular album? Or you recently heard an interesting track on the radio? Alternatively, perhaps the song hasn't yet been created—it lives inside you as a sensation. You don't need to be a musician to work with the magick of this card; in fact, you don't even have to have a particularly strong interest in music as a creative expression. Within this deck, the Music card signals the dynamic link between sound and emotion, and this, of course, emerges in myriad ways. It's the auditory expressions of excitement, passion, and pleasure, along with disappointment, rage, and sorrow. The Music card invites you to define your energetic landscape through noise, which, in turn, may enable you to explore your musical taste and preferences from a deeper, more spiritual point of view. What's more, when the Music card appears, it's likely that the answer you've been seeking will appear through song, so be sure to listen closely. Whether this message is delivered via radio waves or an infectious fifteen-second viral dance video on social media, the presence is deliberately divine. When in doubt, call upon guidance in the form of a familiar name.

THERE ARE NO COINCIDENCES

CARD 39. GEOMETRY   CATEGORY CHANCE

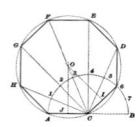

KEYWORDS

Patterns
Formations
Structures
Environments

TANC

Circles
Pyramids
Hexagons
Mandalas
Spiderwebs

PERSONAL NOTES

❖ STORY ❖

GEOMETRY EXISTS ACROSS EVERY DIMENSION——it's spiral galaxies, hexagon beehives, pyramid tombs. Geometry is one of the oldest branches of mathematics and is the core of physics, engineering, and architecture. Within the metaphysical realm, geometry offers profound mysticism that corresponds with our perception of boundaries, cyclicality, spirit, and matter. "Sacred geometry" is the ancient, esoteric tradition of linking shapes to divinity, exploring the esoteric significance of recurring patterns (for instance, the phenomenon of the "golden spiral"——also referred to as the logarithmic spiral or Fibonacci sequence——is often explored through both a scientific and spiritual perspective). Indeed, geometry consists of organic and inorganic spatial organizations that function as containers, delineating form and function. This is expressed in language as well: The "inner circle" offers access to an exclusive closeness, while a "love triangle" connotes challenging romantic dynamics. But do we project our consciousness on shapes and forms, or does consciousness mirror the dynamic geometric patterns embedded into both the physical and astral dimensions? This spatial phenomenon is nothing short of sublime.

❖ INTERPRETATION ❖

When the Geometry card appears, consider how shapes, lines, angles, and forms appear in your life. From an astrological perspective, geometry may manifest through the connection formed between planets and celestial bodies. Likewise, the Geometry card may show up to signal important astrological activity: Explore your birth chart, check your horoscope, or simply catch up on the daily astro-weather. What's going on in the cosmos? Alternatively, the Geometry card might also emerge to encourage a shift in your emotional or physical environment. Perhaps your thinking has been too circular——in that case, the Geometry card will invite you to punctuate this shape by approaching the situation from a different point of view. Or maybe it's time to direct your attention to your habitat: Adjust wall art that's slightly askew. Create symmetry at your workstation. Geometry is mathematics, but it's also experiential: Just like the modern architecture axiom "form follows function," remember that you are a cosmic pattern, too.

CARD 40. NUMBERS   CATEGORY CHANCE

KEYWORDS

Alignments
Manifestations
Purpose
Refinement

TANC

Timestamps
Addresses
Pages
License Plates
Speed Limits

PERSONAL NOTES

❧ STORY ❧

IN THE METAPHYSICAL DOMAIN, numbers are more than expressions of quantities. Numbers are patterns, messages, vibrations. Numbers are representations of energy and life force and divinity——they're tools regularly employed by guides, angels, ancestors, and higher powers to offer wisdom, insight, instruction, and direction. Numerologists use simple arithmetic to derive the "root number" (traditionally 1 through 9, along with 11 and 22) from phone numbers, business addresses, and calendar dates, unlocking the core themes associated with each entity (detailed on page X in this guidebook). But numbers' spiritual significance——on an individual level——transcends any predetermined formula. Indeed, esoteric teachings in Kabbalah associate 11:11 with tetragrammaton, God's unpronounceable four-letter name (יהוה), underscoring the profound sanctity of numerical sequences. Experiencing numbers as symbols unlocks a higher state of consciousness, empowering you to move beyond your existing circumstances and into the realm of infinite possibilities.

❧ INTERPRETATION ❧

What's the time? What's the temperature? What's your phone's battery percentage? When this card appears, take a moment to scan your environment, observing numbers that show up in the even the most ordinary places. The Numbers card signals alignment, harmony, and connectivity——this card indicates that you will be receiving important information on both a quantitative and qualitative level. However, while a quick Google search will certainly yield insight on hundreds of number combinations, the Numbers card in this deck invites you to first look inward, fortifying a personal connection with these divine figures before seeking outward confirmation. What do these numerical patterns mean to you? What do they signify in your unique reality? Are they a sign that you should continue on your path? To keep pushing forward against all odds? Or perhaps the presence of Numbers is an invitation to slow down, prioritize rest, and focus on more restorative expressions? When the Numbers card emerges, you're presented with a powerful opportunity to define your connection to this dynamic spiritual language. This is your reality, so don't be afraid to make the rules.

THERE ARE NO COINCIDENCES

CARD 41. NAMES   CATEGORY CHANCE

KEYWORDS

❖

Identity
Value
Reputation
Legacy

❖

TANC

❖

Avatars
Usernames
Surnames
Titles
Pseudonyms

❖

PERSONAL NOTES

❖ STORY ❖

IN SHAKESPEARE'S LEGENDARY TRAGEDY OF star-crossed lovers, Juliet famously muses—*that which we call a rose, by any other name would smell as sweet*—exploring how titles exist independently from an entity's intrinsic value. Names are deeply codified signifiers that—depending on environment, context, country, culture, and language—quickly communicate tons of complex information about nationality, heritage, gender, religion, and countless other social associations. As such incredibly loaded designations, we may change names to better reflect our identity, adopt the surname of a spouse, or swap letters for images to challenge the limitations of alphabetical symbols. But names aren't just intended for people: Everything is assigned a word, which means titling is an expression of understanding. In fact, many psychologists recommend the practice of naming emotions to help identify complex nonphysical expressions. So, whether we are referring to a person, place, or thing, names carry more weight than just a sequence of letters or characters—names establish existence.

❖ INTERPRETATION ❖

When this card appears, keep an eye out for names. Maybe you'll notice a grandparent's name in an unexpected place? Or perhaps an unfamiliar name is appearing repeatedly, but you're not quite sure why you're aware of this pattern? In the metaphysical realm where there are no coincidences, you can be sure that there is a method to the madness: The Names card indicates that you're receiving messages through titles. Even observing the same name multiple times—regardless of whether it's associated with anyone you know personally—is a powerful indication that your movements are spiritually supported. It may end up manifesting quite literally (perhaps it's the name of your future romantic partner), but it's possible that the names you encounter will remain mysterious, ineffable breadcrumbs— and that's fantastic, too. After all, real magick cannot always be explained: Is that the name of a distant ancestor, many generations removed? Or perhaps it was you in a past life, a beautiful mystical nexus that transcends timelines? There are countless reasons that names light your way, but when this card appears, you can guarantee divine intervention. When in doubt, call upon your guidance in the form of a familiar name.

CARD 42. ELIXIRS   CATEGORY CHANCE

KEYWORDS

Temptation
Evasion
Distraction
Denial

TANC

Potions
Fountains
Tinctures
Cheat Codes
Escape Holes

PERSONAL NOTES

❧ STORY ❧

THE TERM *DEUS EX MACHINA*——or "god out of the machine"——originated in ancient Greek theater over two thousand years ago. When a play's plotline became too complicated or exhaustingly tragic, large cranes would be used to fly actors (dressed as deities) onto the stage to "fix" the unsolvable problems, absolve characters, and bring the tale to a happy ending. Ta-da! Of course, from a literary perspective, deus ex machina was highly frowned upon; plays that employed this technique in earnest were considered ill-structured and lacking creative cohesion. This may be true, but perhaps this technique isn't intended to mirror reality, but rather reflect our deep, relentless desire for a magickal elixir. While this type of supernatural remedy would certainly be astounding, the symbolic implications of a cure-all are distinctly different from a miracle: Elixirs function as shortcuts that are often used to evade responsibility. Likewise, the allegorical elixir——like the deus ex machina——can be quite dubious. Sure, your worries and troubles may suddenly evaporate . . . but at what cost? You may end up with a bad hangover, a soiled reputation, or something much more severe, so when offered an elixir, remember that all actions have consequences.

❧ INTERPRETATION ❧

The Elixirs card is certainly evocative——after all, it usually appears when you're already under a great deal of stress. Whether you're juggling tons of responsibilities, navigating complex interpersonal dynamics, or looking for answers in a liminal space, it's likely that you're desperately seeking your own deus ex machina. How will these situations be resolved? The Elixirs card indicates that you need reprieve. Perhaps it's a vacation, a mental health day, or simply switching your phone off for a few hours. When used in moderation, the Elixirs card can offer a much-needed temporary distraction, allowing you to release tension and revisit your circumstances from a broader perspective. However, the presence of the Elixirs card may also suggest escapism, delusion, or even deception. Indeed, the appearance of this card demands honesty: Are you *really* being truthful, or is there something——or someone——you're intentionally avoiding? It may be tempting to sip the elixir but, don't forget, no quick-fix lasts forever.

THERE ARE NO COINCIDENCES

CARD 43. INTUITION   CATEGORY CHANCE

KEYWORDS

❖

Protection
Security
Confidence
Revelation

❖

TANC

❖

Vibrations
Energy
Tingles
Feelings
Hints

❖

PERSONAL NOTES

❖ STORY ❖

INTUITION IS BAKED INTO EVERY CARD in this deck——in fact, TANC is animated by this dynamic inner knowing. As we begin to dip our toes into the metaphysical domain, we call upon innate wisdom that is deeper and more magnetically expansive than we could have ever imagined possible. But one question I'm frequently asked is how to distinguish anxiety from intuition——since they both entail a type of internal dialogue, how can they be differentiated? This, fortunately, has an answer: Anxiety is a siren, while intuition is a whisper. Anxiety swirls, spirals, and cascades——loud and abrasive, it usually arrives in direct response to an external circumstance and works extremely hard to legitimize its assertions to camouflage itself as intuition. And then there's intuition. Quiet, austere, and effortlessly confident, intuition does not bother justifying its presence——it simply *exists*. Intuition doesn't need to kick and scream to get your attention. It will appear as a breeze, glimmer, or twinkle. Regardless of the message it delivers, intuition will often feel grounding, stabilizing, and centering: Intuition is your ally. Of course, it takes time, practice, and patience to harness your intuition, but that's the case with everything magickal and mundane. The first step, of course, is saying hello.

❖ INTERPRETATION ❖

For seasoned spiritual practitioners, the presence of the Intuition card is clear and straightforward: This is an invitation to connect with your inner knowing. In a way, this card has a bit of a cheeky tone, as if to say, "Hey, why you asking me? You already have the answer." The Intuition card is a concentrated expression of your own innate wisdom. However, if you're still relatively new to this work——the Intuition card may inspire a spiritual exercise. Close your eyes and ask your higher self for a sign, image, word, or color to illuminate this moment. Once you can identify the signifier, hold that symbol in your mind's eye and ask yourself what it means. Why would that particular symbol be relevant for you right now? What does it want you to know? By working with the Intuition card and strengthening your own internal feedback loop, you'll become increasingly comfortable working with this deck. At the end of the day, intuition is the foundation of magick.

CARD 44. MIRACLES   CATEGORY CHANCE

KEYWORDS

❖

Devotion
Alchemy
Hope
Divinity

❖

TANC

❖

Rainbows
Shooting Stars
Aurora
Borealis
Biolumines-
cence
Recovery

❖

PERSONAL NOTES

❖ STORY ❖

DURING A PARTICULARLY THORNY FAMILY CRISIS
several years ago, my anxiety——a familiar siren I've known since childhood——was wailing at a truly insufferable volume. I started asking friends and colleagues for expert recommendations and received the name of a highly regarded hypnotherapist. As I logged in for our virtual session, I explained my situation, elucidating my current stresses and fears. After sharing my story, she looked at me through the screen: "Well, it sounds like you need a miracle." I laughed. But she didn't. She leaned closer to the computer and, with a furrowed brow, asked me if I believed in miracles: "This isn't about religion. It's about creating space for the impossible, because the impossible happens all the time." And all these years later——I'm still pondering those words. She was right. Miracles happen every single day. They may not always take form as the cinematic "near-death" experiences portrayed in movies, but—— when you start paying attention——miracles are absolutely every-where. Tucked in corners of memories and exhaled with every breath, consciousness is animated by miracles..

❖ INTERPRETATION ❖

The Miracles card is the anchor of this deck; it's why signs, sym-bols, and messages appear in the form of cosmos, nature, thresh-olds, and chances. It's your consciousness that exists right now, at this moment, in this form. And it is perfect. The Miracles card manifests literally——though its form may not always be straight-forward. In fact, sometimes the most tremendous, life-altering marvels can first present as disappointment, rejection, or even betrayal. But difficulties and miracles are not mutually exclusive; in fact, they often pair together in perfect poeticism because you——and only you——know that specific flavor of existence that defines your narrative. Perhaps the miracle is the alchemy: the ability to transform those most challenging circumstances into divine inspiration. The Miracles card reveals the power of possibilities baked into everything, both monumental and minus-cule. When this card appears, don't be afraid to suspend disbelief: Nothing is impossible.

THERE ARE NO COINCIDENCES   ·   79

EDITOR:
SAMANTHA WEINER

DESIGN MANAGER:
DIANE SHAW

MANAGING EDITOR:
GLENN RAMIREZ

PRODUCTION MANAGER:
KATHLEEN GAFFNEY

DESIGN:
SEBIT MIN

ISBN: 978-1-4197-6475-2
eISBN: 978-1-64700-868-0

Text copyright © 2022 Aliza Kelly
Illustrations/photographs copyright © 2022

Box and cover © 2022 Abrams

Published in 2022 by Abrams Image, an imprint of ABRAMS. All rights reserved. No portion of this book may be reproduced, stored in a retrieval system, or transmitted in any form or by any means, mechanical, electronic, photocopying, recording, or otherwise, without written permission from the publisher.

Printed and bound in China
10 9 8 7 6 5 4 3 2 1

Abrams Image books are available at special discounts when purchased in quantity for premiums and promotions as well as fundraising or educational use. Special editions can also be created to specification. For details, contact specialsales@abramsbooks.com or the address below.

Abrams Image® is a registered trademark of Harry N. Abrams, Inc.

ART CREDITS
Box cover, guidebook cover, page 1: *Vignettes début de siècle: Attributs de commerce, Culs-de-lampe, Allégories, Passepartout, Sujets divers* by Collectif (Inter-Livres, 1987); local_doctor / Shutterstock; **pages 1, 2, 16, 18, 20, 32, 34, 36, 48, 50, 52, 64, 66, 68:** Lenny Tam / EyeEm / Getty Images; **page 5:** iStock.com / THEPALMER; **page 6:** Channarong Pherngjanda / Shutterstock; **pages 7, 17, 58, 74; cards 28, 39:** Morphart Creation / Shutterstock; **pages 10, 47, 63, 65, 70, 79; cards 22, 33, 35, 44:** iStock.com / ilbusca; **pages 18, 31; cards 2, 11:** mikroman6 / Moment / Getty Images; **page 21:** Patrick Guenette / Alamy Stock Vector; **page 23; card 3:** Pavel Kusmartsev / Alamy Stock Photo; **pages 24, 25, 26, 27, 28, 29, 30; cards 4, 5, 6, 7, 8, 9, 10:** Vlada Young / Shutterstock; **page 37; card 12:** iStock.com / pikepicture; **page 38; card 13:** iStock.com / Nastasic; **page 39; card 14:** iStock.com / Vladi333; **page 40; card 15:** Old Images / Alamy Stock Photo; **page 41; card 16:** iStock.com / Grafissimo; **page 42; card 17:** From *Pictorial Archive of Printer's Ornaments: From the Renaissance to the 20th Century* edited by Carol Belanger Graton (Dover Publications, 1980); **page 44; card 19:** ilbusca / DigitalVision Vectors / Getty Images; **pages 45, 53, 71, 72; cards 20, 23, 36, 37:** From *Scan This Book Two* by John Mendenhall (Art Direction Book Co, 1996); **page 46; card 21:** iStock.com / GeorgePeters; **page 54; card 24:** From *Picture Sourcebook for Collage and Decoupage* edited by Edmund V. Gillon, Jr. (Dover Publications, 1974); **pages 55, 56, 76; cards 25, 26, 41:** From *Scan This Book* edited by John Mendenhall (Art Direction Book Co, 1991); **page 59; card 29:** iStock.com / channarongsds; **page 60; card 30:** Alexander_P / Shutterstock; **page 61; card 31:** Luminarium Graphics; **page 62; card 32:** DELstudio / Shutterstock; **page 73; card 38:** iStock.com / ivan-96; **page 75; card 40:** iStock.com / NSA Digital Archive

ABRAMS The Art of Books
195 Broadway, New York, NY 10007
abramsbooks.com